Praise for *The Words of the Witch*

"*The Words of the Witch* masterfully unveils the impact of language in magickal practices. This well-researched book delves into the historical and practical aspects of spoken and written magick, making it a rich resource for beginners and experienced practitioners alike. Grant provides detailed insights into crafting spells and incantations and selecting magickal alphabets. Her exploration of rhyme, rhythm, and word choice is both deep and clear, enhanced by practical exercises. This work, a magickal journey into the heart of word magick, shines with the author's expertise and enthusiasm, establishing it as an essential addition to any magickal library."

—**MAT AURYN**, bestselling author of *Psychic Witch*

"Smart, stylish, and sophisticated, *The Words of the Witch* is a clever guide for witches, Pagans, and magicians of all levels and experience who wish to create their own magickal writings. Here you will learn how to successfully write spells, prayers, mantras, blessings, invocations, quarter calls, and much more! Grant's background as an English and creative writing professor truly shines through as she teaches you some of the history behind spell writing, the power of the spoken and written word, as well as the mechanics of composition. Grant explains everything you'll need to know to accomplish your personal magickal writing goals, and she even includes some hands-on projects to get your creative juices flowing. If you want to advance your Craft, this is the book to read!"

—**ELLEN DUGAN**, author of *Natural Witchery*

"This book will guide you to a more transformative practice by exploring the power of language. The reader will find lessons exploring magical writing, sound, poetry, chants, and more. You'll find a collection of exercises and projects that are sure to delight your natural urge to express yourself magically. Although not a beginner book, it is very accessible and written with wisdom and warmth. Ember Grant has done it again; *The Words of the Witch* is a must-have for your witchcraft bookshelf!"

—**MICKIE MUELLER**, author of *The Witch's Mirror* and
  Llewellyn's Little Book of Halloween

the Words of the Witch

About the Author

Ember Grant is a full-time English professor and teaches writing, poetry, and literature. She has been writing for Llewellyn for more than twenty years and is the author of numerous articles and four books: *Mythology for a Magical Life*, *The Book of Crystal Spells*, *The Second Book of Crystal Spells*, and *Magical Candle Crafting*. Follow her on Instagram: @poetofthewoods.

the Words of the Witch

of the

Witch

Writing and Speaking Your Magic

Ember Grant

LLEWELLYN
WOODBURY, MINNESOTA

FIRST EDITION
First Printing, 2024

Book design by R. Brasington
Cover design by Kevin R. Brown
Interior illustrations by Llewellyn Art Department

Llewellyn Publications is a registered trademark of Llewellyn Worldwide Ltd.

Library of Congress Cataloging-in-Publication Data
Names: Grant, Ember, author.
Title: The words of the witch : writing and speaking your magic / Ember
    Grant.
Description: First edition. | Woodbury, Minnesota : Llewellyn Publications,
    2024. | Includes bibliographical references and index. | Summary: "This
    well-researched and engaging book provides everything you need to
    maximize one of your most powerful sources of magic: language. Sharing
    more than thirty practices and projects, Ember Grant teaches you how to
    manifest your goals through written and spoken magic"—Provided by
    publisher.
Identifiers: LCCN 2024034797 (print) | LCCN 2024034798 (ebook) | ISBN
    9780738774176 | ISBN 9780738774305 (ebook)
Subjects: LCSH: Magic. | Witchcraft. | Language and languages—Miscellanea.
Classification: LCC BF1621 .G687 2024 (print) | LCC BF1621 (ebook) | DDC
    133.4/4—dc23/eng/20240924
LC record available at https://lccn.loc.gov/2024034797
LC ebook record available at https://lccn.loc.gov/2024034798

Llewellyn Publications
A Division of Llewellyn Worldwide Ltd.
2143 Wooddale Drive
Woodbury, MN 55125-2989
www.llewellyn.com

Printed in the United States of America

Other Books by Ember Grant

Magical Candle Crafting

The Book of Crystal Spells

The Second Book of Crystal Spells

Mythology for a Magical Life

Disclaimer

Please use appropriate caution when working with essential oils and other products that are applied to the skin. Always follow product instructions carefully.

For my husband,
whose words inspired this project.

Contents

Part 1: Historical Background

Part 2: The Practice of Spoken Magic

Part 3: The Practice of Written Magic

Part 4: Everything Else

Exercises and Projects

Introduction

"The limits of my language mean the limits of my world."
Ludwig Wittgenstein, *Tractatus Logico-Philosophicus*

When we picture witches and wizards of fantasy, fairy tales, and popular imagination, they are often waving wands, gesturing, maybe hovering over a cauldron or mixing potions. But no matter what action they're taking, they're almost always chanting, whispering, or even shouting incantations, or consulting an ancient grimoire of secret knowledge. In short, they're using language.

Whether by speaking or writing, words have always been the most popular and significant way to make magic happen. Magic workers of ancient times might chant or murmur over someone or breathe words upon a person or object, speak to someone directly, or let the wind carry the words. Attitudes about the words used in magic have run the spectrum from being "merely instruments of persuasion, supplication, or command" to believing the actual words contained magical power.[1] But one thing is certain—words were believed to hold great power in the practice of magic, in all its forms. Language

---

1. Richard Kieckhefer, *Magic in the Middle Ages*, 3rd ed. (Cambridge, UK: Cambridge University Press, 2022), Kindle.

has been regarded as so influential that at one time in history, just knowing another language could lead to someone being accused of witchcraft.[2]

Right now you are viewing, either on paper or on a screen, a collection of little characters that we know as letters, which represent sounds. The combinations make up words, and words link together to make sentences. Sentences come together to make meaning that we understand. It's quite amazing. And we often take it for granted.

Language is what makes us special as human beings—it sets us apart from all other life forms on earth. Sure, other beings can communicate, but our complex system is beyond comparison for what it can accomplish. Even cultures that have no written form of language still communicate with words. Our lives are intertwined with language—it's how we make meaning and understand everything around us. It's how we learn and share information. But there is also the long-held belief by some that certain words have an inherent power, especially in a religious context. Language and writing were once considered by some cultures to be sacred gifts from the gods.

There's no denying the profoundly transformative power of language. Writing and speech have the ability to convince and persuade, to lift hearts, minds, and spirits. Words can also deceive, belittle, cause enduring pain, ruin lives, and damage reputations. When we communicate, we can encourage and empathize, undermine, or challenge. Words also transport us through story and song; they convey information, inspire ideas, and evoke powerful emotions. The possibilities are endless.

This isn't new information. We all know a simple word of kindness can make a world of difference, just as a word of hate can cause irreparable harm. And we can't begin this journey without mentioning that old rhyme about sticks and stones—and acknowledging that it's wrong. Words hurt. Even if we try to tell ourselves otherwise—that what someone says about us doesn't matter, even if we train ourselves to not be bothered by idle comments, enough of them can take their toll. And now more than any time in history, it is so easy to talk about others and spread lies and misinformation. Words can truly do damage. In extreme examples—such as brainwashing and cults—they can cause great harm. If you've ever been called a derogatory name or had something

---

2. Susannah Marriott, *Witches, Sirens and Soothsayers* (London: Spruce Books, 2008), 217.

written about you that was negative or hurtful—a lie told, or a misunderstanding—you know the power of words. If you've ever said (or wrote) something you wished you could take back, you understand that once uttered, words are out of your control, released into the world and universe. One false statement can ruin a reputation or first impression. But, thankfully, they have the power to do as much good. They can empower and inspire us; they can encourage, comfort, and support. One kind word can change someone's life. It's not even magic; it's the simple power of words, and we must not undervalue or underestimate their significance. Knowing this, we should feel extra awe for the power of words in our magical practice.

Whether you identify as a witch, Wiccan, Pagan, magician, or something else, if you practice any type of magic—ceremonial or folk, a specific tradition, even religious magic—you likely use words a great deal in the form of spells, prayers, incantations, evocations, affirmations, and even mantras.[3] Beyond the strength of your will and intent, words are the next most powerful tool you have for magic. In our roles as modern witches and magical practitioners, our words—how and what we say in our magical practices (and in our mundane lives too)—deserve some attention. In reclaiming the word *witch*, we have a responsibility to do this. Just look at the word *witch* itself—a word that many of us embody as a person of benevolent power and wisdom, a healer. At one time in history, calling someone that word could be a death sentence.

As modern witches, we cultivate a life connected to nature and the entire universe. We seek healing and harmony and to defend ourselves and others when necessary. We practice the Craft of the wise, and we never stop learning and seeking to better ourselves and our world, and so our words need to be carefully crafted with intent and sincerity to help us engage with the world and with others and convey our magic. We need to be able to precisely articulate our intent and convey that intent with confidence, to back up our words with belief, even when using words someone else has written. We make them our own by speaking them.

And so I invite you to spend some time in the study of words. While this is certainly not a new subject, and I am not the first to approach the topic in this manner, my goal is to give you ideas for expanding and strengthening

---

3. In this book, I am assuming the reader already has a basic understanding of magical practices, whether folk magic, ceremonial, or both, so I will not be addressing that here.

your use of words in magic (or *magick*, if you prefer), both written and spoken. Even though I'm addressing this to the modern witch, this book is for anyone who practices any type of magic. Even if you're already a master, there is always more to discover. My goal is not to overwhelm you with too much history or linguistics—while such inquiries are fascinating, there are already excellent books on these subjects. My purpose is to bring together a variety of techniques you can use to make the most of your words in order to make your magical expressions more meaningful and effective. So while some of the information here may not be new to you, I hope that you find some fresh approaches and gain a deeper insight into the use of language.

We all know these statements: "A picture is worth a thousand words" and "Actions speak louder than words." I'm not saying these aren't true, but they are a bit dismissive of the power that words hold. Magical practice involves all these aspects—we use images and symbols, actions and gestures, and yes, words. In this book, I've pulled together a variety of strategies and ideas to make the most of how you're using your words. When we speak our intent to the universe, or write it, we plant a seed we wish to manifest. It's like a promise or a vow. It's a "bridge" between "mind and matter."[4] So make your words count. Words have power, and the words of the witch can have even more when the full intent and strength of will support each letter written, each syllable spoken. When you believe this, you can change yourself and the world.

How to Use This Book

It's useful to keep in mind how magic has been understood throughout history—and it's a messy history, filled with complexities, shadowy gray areas, overlap and inconsistencies, and a variety of influences. To that end, part 1 of this book contains a bit of historical context related to spoken and written magic. There is also a special section on talismans and amulets, since these have been, historically speaking, the most popular forms of magic.

Part 2 concerns the use of spoken-word magic. This section of the book contains a variety of skills that can be applied to composing prayers, spells, and more—pieces intended to be spoken or recited. Techniques such as rhyme,

---

4. Patrick Dunn, *Magic, Power, Language, and Symbol: A Magician's Exploration of Linguistics* (Woodbury, MN: Llewellyn Publications, 2008), Kindle.

rhythm, and word choice are explored, in addition to the act of speaking, sound frequency, and other considerations. Examples of the various writing strategies are provided.

In part 3, we explore various forms of written magic. Obviously there will be some overlap between the discussion of spoken and written magic because we typically "write" things meant to be spoken aloud. But this section of the book focuses on the actual writing implements and surfaces—from simple pen and paper to materials such as wood, clay, and glass. In addition, there are practice exercises, hands-on projects, and detailed explanations and recipes for making paper, ink, and more.

Part 4 addresses names, numerology, and formal poetic verse, and part five contains a section on Elements and some practical aspects, including checklists for creating spells, rituals, and other pieces. While it's certainly fine to jump around throughout the book, moving through the material in sequence is recommended since the information builds upon previous chapters. Becoming an experienced word witch means mastering your use of words in all situations.

I don't pretend to be the first to write a book about magical words and language. What I hope to do is add to that discussion and extend the conversation by adding some ideas and more avenues of exploration. As a writer, poet, and English professor (and one who seeks to reclaim the word *witch* as the powerful and nurturing wise-woman archetype), words are my life, and I invite you to join me on a journey of word magic. I hope you find some inspiration along the way.

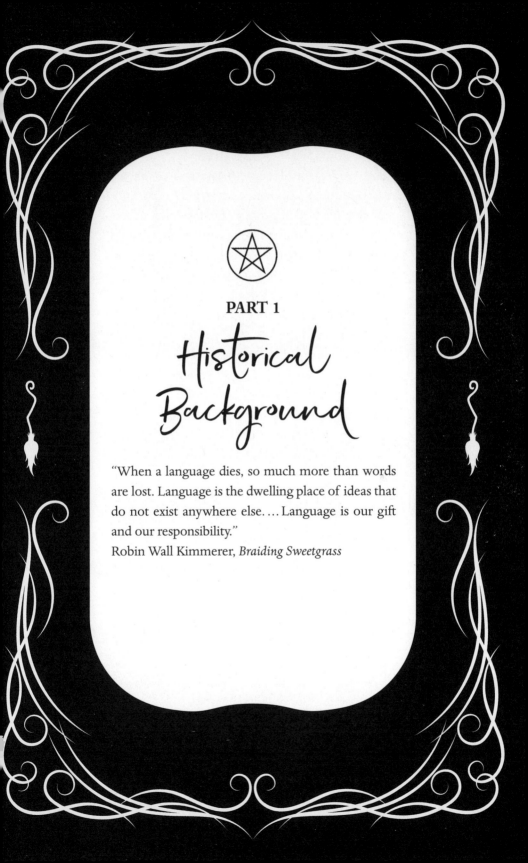

PART 1

Historical Background

"When a language dies, so much more than words are lost. Language is the dwelling place of ideas that do not exist anywhere else. … Language is our gift and our responsibility."

Robin Wall Kimmerer, *Braiding Sweetgrass*

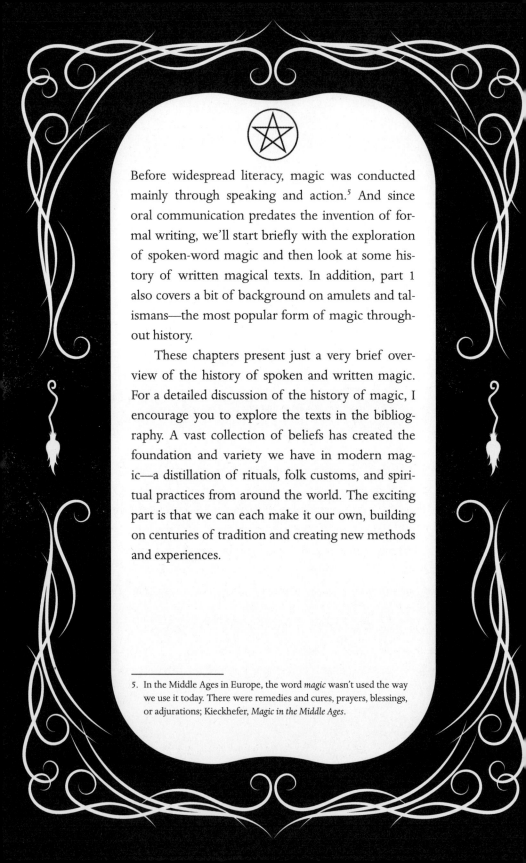

Before widespread literacy, magic was conducted mainly through speaking and action.[5] And since oral communication predates the invention of formal writing, we'll start briefly with the exploration of spoken-word magic and then look at some history of written magical texts. In addition, part 1 also covers a bit of background on amulets and talismans—the most popular form of magic throughout history.

These chapters present just a very brief overview of the history of spoken and written magic. For a detailed discussion of the history of magic, I encourage you to explore the texts in the bibliography. A vast collection of beliefs has created the foundation and variety we have in modern magic—a distillation of rituals, folk customs, and spiritual practices from around the world. The exciting part is that we can each make it our own, building on centuries of tradition and creating new methods and experiences.

---

5. In the Middle Ages in Europe, the word *magic* wasn't used the way we use it today. There were remedies and cures, prayers, blessings, or adjurations; Kieckhefer, *Magic in the Middle Ages*.

CHAPTER 1

Spoken Magic
A Brief History

"A word has power in and of itself. It comes from nothing into sound and meaning; it gives origin to all things."
N. Scott Momaday, *The Way to Rainy Mountain*

Our modern magical practices are a blend of things already syncretized centuries ago, including traditional beliefs and techniques from all over the world—a combination of religious texts, folk customs, and complex rituals of ceremonial magic.[6] Western magic has drawn influence from a variety of regions, but ancient Egypt has long been considered the source of the most proficient magician-priests; their influence was eventually embraced by the Greeks, Romans, Christians, Jews, and, later, Muslims. While words as the source of magic can be found in nearly every culture, some of the most interesting evidence we have is Egyptian.[7]

Since the impact of words is so profound, let's take a moment to look at their importance in ancient Egypt. One of the most interesting aspects is the Egyptians' concept of *heka*, "the animating and controlling force of the universe,"

---

6. Ronald Hutton, *Queens of the Wild: Pagan Goddesses in Christian Europe: An Investigation* (New Haven: Yale University Press, 2022), Kindle.

7. Owen Davies, *Grimoires: A History of Magic Books* (New York: Oxford University Press, 2009), Kindle.

which is one of the most fundamental aspects of Egyptian magic.[8] According to Spell 261 from the *Coffin Texts*, heka "was regarded as the magical vitality which infused the first creative utterance of the solar deity Ra at the birth of the world and which continues to do so at its re-creation every morning with each sunrise."[9] Heka is, in simple terms, the personification of magic (and is sometimes depicted as a deity), and even though it was expressed in speech, writing, and rituals, it was, above all, linked especially to speech and the power of the word.[10] In "Egyptian magic, actions did not necessarily speak louder than words—they were often one and the same thing. Thought, deed, image, and power are theoretically united in the concept of *heka*."[11]

The ancient Egyptians believed so strongly in the creative power of words that the mere utterance of a word or name could bring an object into existence. Phrases such as "'magic of their mouths' and 'spells of their utterances'" reveal the significant relationship between magic and the spoken word.[12] Additionally, it was believed that the goddess Isis "possessed words of power."[13] It was said that she held the secrets of "pronunciation, tone of voice, gestures and timing that compel all living things to stop, listen and do as she bids." Those who knew her "words of power" could receive her protection in the underworld.[14] Even though the written versions were believed to be just as effective, the spells that make up the Egyptian *Book of the Dead* were intended to be recited in order to aid souls in their journey to the afterlife.[15]

We can gain valuable insight about the use of language in magic from the ancient Egyptians. There is a world of significance in the belief that words have

---

8. Ronald Hutton, *The Witch: A History of Fear, from Ancient Times to the Present* (New Haven, CT: Yale University Press, 2017), Kindle.

9. Peter Maxwell-Stuart, "Magic in the Ancient World," in *The Oxford Illustrated History of Witchcraft and Magic*, ed. Owen Davies (Oxford, UK: Oxford University Press, 2017), 5–6.

10. Hutton, *The Witch*.

11. *The Egyptian Book of the Dead: The Book of Going Forth by Day: The Complete Papyrus of Ani Featuring Integrated Text and Full-Color Images*, revised edition, Ogden Goelet Jr., Daniel Gunther, Carol A. R. Andrews, James Wasserman, and Raymond O. Faulkner (San Francisco: Chronicle Books, 2015), 156.

12. Helen Strudwick, ed., *The Encyclopedia of Ancient Egypt* (New York: Metro Books, 2006), 476; Maxwell-Stuart, "Magic in the Ancient World," 6.

13. E. A. Wallis Budge, "The Legend of Ra and Isis," in *The Book of the Dead: The Papyrus of Ani*, Sacred Texts, 1895, https://www.sacred-texts.com/egy/ebod/ebod07.htm.

14. Marriott, *Witches, Sirens, and Soothsayers*, 233.

15. Maxwell-Stuart, "Magic in the Ancient World," 5.

such power to create—everything from the world itself to our goals, wishes, and desires. There's a reason these concepts are still valued today; the impact this culture has had on our modern magical practices cannot be denied. But other cultures have influenced us as well.

There is a great deal of evidence for the significance of spoken-word magic from sacred texts, myths, and legends from cultures all over the world. To the ancient Norse, swearing an oath could be an act of magic, "casting a sort of spell to bind oneself in the future."[16] Norse mythology cites, among Odin's many powers, his ability "with words alone to put out fires, calm the seas, and turn the wind in different directions."[17] The Norse concept of magic saw the will as having power over the world as long as it was "channeled through the spoken word"; by writing or speaking the appropriate words, ordinary people could have access to powers held only by the gods.[18]

Of course, religion is yet another source of sacred words and sounds. In Jewish tradition, the Hebrew language has long been considered divine and the letters themselves believed to contain power. The appropriate combination of words, sounds, and letters could be used for various types of magical workings—everything from conjuring spirits to divination. In addition to the use of signs and symbols, "writing was at the heart of medieval Jewish magic, whether in the form of spells, curses, or protective words on amulets."[19] In Hinduism, "the sacred syllable OM is the source of everything that is"; Muslims believe that "the name Allah contains all the qualities that give rise to the Universe," and Christians believe that "'in the beginning was the Word and the Word was with God, and the Word was God.'"[20]

In European folk magic, spoken words were believed to be more powerful than written texts.[21] It was believed that words could channel "the force of the soul" and serve as a conduit between the person performing the act of magic

---

16. Jackson Crawford, *Norse Mythology* (Chantilly, VA: The Teaching Company, 2021), 169.

17. Stephen A. Mitchell, *Witchcraft and Magic in the Nordic Middle Ages* (Philadelphia, PA: University of Pennsylvania Press, 2011), Kindle.

18. Crawford, *Norse Mythology*, 169; 72.

19. *A History of Magic, Witchcraft and the Occult*, ed. Kathryn Hennessy (London: Penguin Random House, 2020), 87–90.

20. Marriott, *Witches, Sirens and Soothsayers*, 220.

21. *A History of Magic, Witchcraft and the Occult*, 92.

and the person or thing being acted upon.[22] Additionally, even the qualities of a sound are associated with the magical power of the words. The word *spell* itself is a good example of this history: its first recorded use to refer to a set of words as enchantment occurred around the 1570s.[23] It's the word we often use for magic, but we know it also means the arrangement of letters and phrases that are spoken or written. But more than just the goal being fulfilled, the formula must be "correctly pronounced."[24] This adds even more weight to the idea of magic words and their function.

There are many superstitions still with us today surrounding the pronunciation of certain words. You're undoubtedly familiar with the folklore prohibition of saying certain words or names (see part 4 for more on names) or the concept of a jinx—used to both describe how saying something out loud could prevent it from happening ("We're going to win this game!" "Shh—don't jinx it!") or by two people saying the same thing at the same time. Similarly, we knock on wood to avoid tempting fate—the notion that by saying something will or won't happen, we're inviting it to actually occur. And we've all seen comedic examples in film and on television of what happens when a magician gets the accent wrong! All these customs are rooted in ancient practices of magic.

And we must not forget that in addition to the cunning folk and practitioners of magic of ages past, bards and storytellers transmitted information and stories orally. In fact, in the ancient Celtic world, bards were revered. Poets were among the few citizens able to "move freely throughout the countryside without needing to ask permission to enter a new territory."[25] Reputation was essential; people in positions of power would commission a poet to sing of their great deeds. On the other hand, a poet could also be hired to perform a satire to smear someone's name. The bard had a significant amount of power,

22. Kieckhefer, *Magic in the Middle Ages*.

23. "Spell," Etymology Online, accessed April 2, 2024, https://www.etymonline.com/word/spell.

24. *Encyclopaedia Britannica: A New Survey of Universal Knowledge*, vol. 21: Sordello to Textile Printing (London: Encyclopaedia Britannica, Ltd., 1929), 201.

25. Jennifer Paxton, *The Celtic World* (Chantilly, VA: The Teaching Company, 2018), 135.

an influence beyond the creation of songs and stories—their actual words were even thought to physically affect their listeners.[26]

And, of course, the realm of spoken-word magic is also the domain of the shaman. Words and sounds work together to create altered states of consciousness. The shamanic figure in certain cultures acts as an intermediary between the mundane world and the spirit realm. The shaman often employs the use of chant to enter trances and commune with other realms—a practice that is still very much alive today in many forms.

---

26. Sharon Paice MacLeod, *Celtic Cosmology and the Otherworld: Mythic Origins, Sovereignty and Liminality* (Jefferson, NC: McFarland & Co., 2018), Kindle.

CHAPTER 2

Written Magic

A Brief History

"The written word was a thing of awe in the days when most people couldn't write, especially if it included holy words."
Susannah Marriott, *Witches, Sirens and Soothsayers*

Ever since the first human marked on a cave wall, we've desired to leave our mark on the world, often just to say, "I was here." We still can't resist. Just consider all the places where you've seen graffiti or someone's message of "wash me" written in the dust on a car.

There is something mysterious and exciting about reading the words of ancient spells found on papyri or pottery or engraved on curse tablets and amulets. While we rarely have complete context for these artifacts, scholars have published a great deal of information about these items, and many of the pieces are on display in museums. Much of our modern magical tradition comes from these ancient artifacts. It's important to keep in mind that all the evidence we have, even to discuss the magic of the spoken word, comes from written texts and engraved or inscribed objects. So now let's explore some of those.

There are many theories about how the practice of writing emerged. Many believe it began with pictograms—symbols, like little pictures, that represented objects. Some scholars say it was a discovery made intentionally through practice; others believe it was an accident. Another popular theory is that it evolved over time in each culture because people simply needed to keep records, and counting became insufficient to organize everything.[27] According to Mark Zender, it's most likely that writing developed independently in ancient cultures, mainly, at first, to denote ownership of things and express titles and names. It proved to be such a useful tool that it was expanded for other uses.[28]

The earliest form of writing is the cuneiform script of ancient Mesopotamia. *Cuneiform* means "wedge-shaped" and refers to the shape of the wooden stylus used to make marks on clay tablets. The oldest Egyptian writing dates soon after, followed by writing from the Indus Valley, Crete, China, and Central America.[29] Even though there is no solid evidence to definitively prove if individual civilizations each came up with their own systems independently or if the idea spread from one source to others (most likely a combination of both), there's no doubt that borrowing occurred, and it continues today. Living languages change and grow along with civilizations that use them.

One thing we do know is that, for magical use, whether words were spoken or written made a difference. One reason spoken magic was so powerful is that there would have been a psychological effect created by the combination of words, gestures, and objects used to "perform" a spell. However, written words could still be effective, and there was a belief that something inscribed may last longer, that the power could endure.[30] To the ancient Norse, the written word was believed to have even more power than spoken words. While most runic inscriptions were mundane, the runes could be used to make an incantation "permanent" on something like bone, wood, stone, or metal. However, ultimately, it was the content, not the actual shape of the word that was important.[31]

Much of our evidence about magical practice comes from the Greek magical papyri. These are sheets of papyrus that contain magical writing—including magical spells, hymns, and rituals—in Greek or in the Demotic language of Egypt. Most of these artifacts date from the second century BCE to the fifth

---

27. Andrew Robinson, *The Story of Writing*, 2nd ed. (London: Thames and Hudson, 2020), 11.

28. Marc Zender, *Writing and Civilization: From Ancient Worlds to Modernity* (Chantilly, VA: The Teaching Company, 2013), 19.

29. Robinson, *The Story of Writing*, 12.

30. Kieckhefer, *Magic in the Middle Ages*.

31. Crawford, *Norse Mythology*, 170–71.

century CE. These documents only represent a small portion of what once existed, but we also have artifacts to help with interpretation.[32]

The myths and sacred teachings of many cultures profess the belief that words and writing are divine, and many have specific directions and guidelines for their use. Again we turn to the ancient Egyptians, who may be the most famous for this. They believed writing was a gift from the god Thoth—a gift they were responsible for using with great care because words were powerful and had the potential to both help and harm.[33] Many phonetic characters also have significance meaning beyond their literal interpretation—either magical or symbolic.[34] According to Egyptologist Rosalie David, "the main purpose of writing was not decorative, and it was not originally intended for literary or commercial use. Its most important function was to provide a means by which certain concepts or events could be brought into existence. The Egyptians believed that if something were committed to writing it could be repeatedly 'made to happen' by means of magic."[35]

Hieroglyph is a Greek word that means "sacred carving," and the evidence from those sacred carvings is extensive: amulets, stone monuments, and inscriptions on metal and clay tablets and bowls. While some of the hiero-glyphic scripts that accompany the reliefs on temple walls are descriptions of activities, it is believed that their original purpose was magical and that inscrib-ing the text on the wall of a temple increased the power of the ritual.[36] In fact, hieroglyphic writing conveyed so much magical force "that pouring water over the characters inscribed on stele or other religious documents would effectively transfer this power to the liquid, allowing magical language to be ingested or otherwise employed by suppliants."[37] And as we know from collections such as the *Coffin Texts* and the *Book of the Dead*, the power of words was so significant

32. Hans Dieter Betz, ed., *The Greek Magical Papyri in Translation*, 2nd ed. (Chicago: University of Chicago Press, 1992), xli.

33. Joshua J. Mark, "Ancient Egyptian Writing," World History Encyclopedia, November 16, 2016, https://www.worldhistory.org/Egyptian_Writing/.

34. Strudwick, ed., *The Encyclopedia of Ancient Egypt*, 481.

35. Rosalie David, *Handbook to Life in Ancient Egypt*, revised edition (New York: Facts on File, 2003), 243–44.

36. Strudwick, *The Encyclopedia of Ancient Egypt*, 498.

37. Andrew T. Wilburn, *Materia Magica: The Archaeology of Magic in Roman Egypt, Cyprus, and Spain* (Ann Arbor, MI: University of Michigan Press, 2016), 69–70.

that knowing certain spells, prayers, and rituals could assure one's safe passage into the afterlife.

The Sumerians believed writing was invented by the god Enlil; the Assyrians and Babylonians borrowed the writing style but believed instead that it was invented by their god Nabu.[38] But unlike the Egyptians, the ancient Mesopotamians didn't believe it was possible to command or coerce their gods. Rather, they were more focused on the influence of celestial bodies, and this is one of the sources for our Western astrological tradition in magic.[39] They also had a strong fear of malevolent spirits that could cause harm. In fact, "Sumerians, Assyrians, and Babylonians all sought help from exorcists and omen-interpreters to gain protection from malign supernatural entities and discover the future."[40] Clay tablets have been found containing incantations, magic spells, and prophecies. But like the ancient Egyptians, they, too, believed that knowing the name of an entity gave power over it.[41] (For more on names, see chapter 16.)

The fact that writing was considered sacred is the main reason so much of it has been preserved over time.[42] Through archaeological research and the discovery of artifacts, the gradual transition from oral magic to written spells can be traced, and as literacy increased, more details were written, revealing these changes. The main textual sources we have for magic spells in the Western world, historically and linguistically speaking, are of three types: (1) Christian liturgy, psalms, prayers, etc., (2) Greek, Hebrew, and Latin words, and (3) sequences of letters that can be the initials of words. Many of the words found on relics and amulets aren't even actual words, but have been altered to emphasize particular sounds. Letters were often used as mnemonics to preserve the secrecy of a phrase, like writing in a secret code.[43] While the textual evidence reveals these three main sources of influence, we must not forget that those sources were, in turn, influenced by practices from the Middle East. The Greeks and Romans were especially fascinated by the beliefs of Mesopotamia and Egypt, and they borrowed many of their traditions, including protective

---

38. Zender, *Writing and Civilization*, 5.

39. Hutton, *The Witch.*

40. *A History of Magic, Witchcraft and the Occult*, 18–19.

41. Hutton, *The Witch.*

42. Zender, *Writing and Civilization*, 6.

43. Claude Lecouteux, *Dictionary of Ancient Magic Words and Spells: From Abraxas to Zoar*, trans. Jon E. Graham (Rochester, VT: Inner Traditions, 2014), Kindle.

counter-magic, necromancy, and a variety of ritual practices.[44] It's interesting to note that while writing was sacred to the ancient Egyptians, the ancient Greeks were ambivalent toward writing, for it could be a means of deception. Plato famously argued that the written word "discouraged the use of memory."[45]

Ironically, though the ancient Romans destroyed a great deal of material, we actually have the Christian church to thank for so many magical texts being preserved, especially books (see the Grimoires section on page 21). While today there are often sharp lines drawn between religion and magic, we know that hasn't always been the case. In fact, early Christians employed the use of textual amulets and engaged in other practices "based on the magical efficacy of written words to protect, exorcise, and cure."[46] In fact, clerics often did work that could lead to accusations of sorcery.[47]

Even as Christianity spread throughout Europe, forcing pagan practices into obscurity, magic still survived. Christian beliefs were blended with folk magic, and many people engaged in these practices, including doctors and clergy, who actually profited from the act of creating and copying spells and charms.[48] In *Dictionary of Ancient Magic Words and Spells*, Claude Lecouteux categorizes these various types of spells as "charms …, orisons [prayers], blessings, conjurations, and medical prescriptions."[49] At first, these charms were given a Christian facade, then Christians created their own "spells" inspired by pagan examples.[50] Much of this magic was in the form of amulets, and Christian amulets were popular in Europe during the Middle Ages. Remember that the acceptance of Christianity didn't happen overnight, and there was a long period of transition where lines between magic and religion were blurred. Magic was part of religion for centuries until a distinction was made between

---

44. Robert Andrew Gilbert and John F. M. Middleton, "History of Magic in Western Worldviews," Encyclopedia Britannica, updated May 3, 2024, https://www.britannica.com/topic/magic-supernatural-phenomenon/History-of-magic-in-Western-worldviews.

45. Wilburn, *Materia Magica*, 69–70.

46. Don C. Skemer, *Binding Words: Textual Amulets in the Middle Ages* (University Park: Pennsylvania State University Press, 2006), 21.

47. Claude Lecouteux, *The High Magic of Talismans and Amulets: Tradition and Craft*, trans. Jon E. Graham (Rochester, VT: Inner Traditions, 2014), Kindle.

48. *A History of Magic, Witchcraft and the Occult*, 92.

49. Lecouteux, *Dictionary of Ancient Magic Words*.

50. Lecouteux, *Dictionary of Ancient Magic Words*.

the permitted "magic" of the church and the "evil" or "demonic" magic done outside it.

There were some scholars during this time of transition who still professed a belief in occult powers, numbers, prophetic dreams, and divination, but eventually the predominant attitude became that magic was a threat, a practice that rivaled the church and prayer.[51] Even when a plant was known to have curative properties, some people still suspected demonic influence. A major shift occurred when magic became defined as either "natural" or "demonic." This was an attitude of the learned elite, but they, too, played fast and loose with definitions. What was referred to as "natural" magic concerned occult or "hidden powers" in nature that were unexplained by the inherent qualities of the item, often influences believed to come from celestial bodies. This was considered "science," and it was a pretty broad definition. Demonic magic, on the other hand, was considered a "perversion of religion." This involved asking for help from entities other than God.[52]

Nearly anything not related to prayer was considered demonic magic, but the most damaging distinction was really made around the sixteenth century to reinforce the notion that "religion … *supplicates* God … and magic … *coerces* spiritual beings or forces."[53] You can see how even this definition could be problematic. What is the exact difference? Most people of the time didn't make this distinction. For example, attitudes of people invoking the name of Christ could "run the gamut from magical incantation at one extreme to mystical piety at the other"; intentions were often ambiguous and complicated.[54] While the Christian church of the Middle Ages condemned pagan magic on one hand while practicing their own type with the other, it's because even they realized there was a gray area—overlap between what was labeled magic and religion. Magic and religion have always been deeply intertwined and cannot be easily separated, despite every attempt to define them. During this time, clerics, monks, and priests continued to produce textual amulets using prayers, the names of saints, and other references to sacred material.[55] Parchment con-

---

51. Kieckhefer, *Magic in the Middle Ages*.

52. Kieckhefer, *Magic in the Middle Ages*.

53. Kieckhefer, *Magic in the Middle Ages*.

54. Kieckhefer, *Magic in the Middle Ages*.

55. Skemer, *Binding Words*, 50.

taining prayers could be rolled and carried for protection and "relics of saints" served as amulets as well.[56] And even though one could obtain religious textual amulets, "urban Christians occasionally could not resist pagan magic."[57] We know the church eventually suppressed pagan worship, but they were never really able to maintain a clear division between "religious devotion and magic."[58]

Books of Magic: Grimoires

The medieval period witnessed a rise in the formation of magical texts, which eventually became known as grimoires. These books were most often written in Latin, but there were some in Arabic or Hebrew.[59] Usually these were only available to the learned elite. However, the church had access to books of remedies and narrative charms. Clergy of the medieval period were often the main practitioners of magic and users of grimoires, and monasteries housed great collections of magical texts.[60] The word *grimoire* is an alteration of "grammaria" ("grammar") and was once used simply to designate a book that was written in Latin. Of course, collections of magical texts existed before this word was used. Grimoires were either small enough to fit in a pocket, or large and intended for display. Early grimoires were written on parchment, which is animal skin. Virgin parchment was sometimes used (*virgin* being skin from an animal that died before reaching sexual maturity) or virgin wax (wax never used for any other purpose). These books of magic began as treatises by medieval authors on various subjects, including the movement and positions of celestial bodies, names of angels and demons, secret symbols, and directions for creating amulets and talismans.[61] They could also be collections of recipes, remedies, rites, rituals, and prayers. There were also medical books that contained cures and remedies, many of which were magical formulas.

---

56. Kieckhefer, *Magic in the Middle Ages*.

57. Skemer, *Binding Words*, 40.

58. Davies, *Grimoires*.

59. *A History of Magic, Witchcraft and the Occult*, 108.

60. Davies, *Grimoires*.

61. Claude Lecouteux, *The Book of Grimoires: The Secret Grammar of Magic*, trans. Jon E. Graham (Rochester, VT: Inner Traditions, 2013), Kindle.

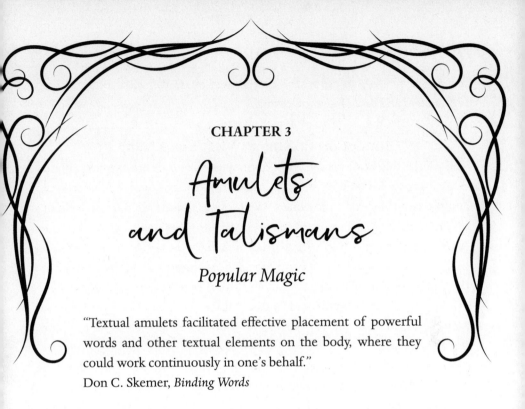

CHAPTER 3

Amulets and Talismans

Popular Magic

"Textual amulets facilitated effective placement of powerful words and other textual elements on the body, where they could work continuously in one's behalf."
Don C. Skemer, *Binding Words*

Of all the various forms of written magic throughout the ages and cultures, amulets are the most common, and they have been found in thousands of forms all over the world in all cultures.[62] In fact, amulets are one of the main sources we have for the practice of magic throughout history. People have used amulets for thousands of years, and the development of the written word not only made previously orally transmitted magic available to more people, but preserved the evidence that survives today.[63] The word *amulet* can be used to describe a wide range of objects—basically anything that served the purpose of the spell. While amulets were often a blend of signs, symbols, numbers, and letters—most of which have lost meaning for us today (the secrecy preserved the magic from being known to others)—textual amulets were extremely popular, especially in the Middle Ages. These amulets contained letters, words, and

62. Lecouteux, *High Magic of Talismans*.

63. Skemer, *Binding Words*, 23.

phrases for a variety of purposes—everything from prayer and exorcism to curing illnesses and providing protection.[64]

Amulet or Talisman: What's in a Name?

The use of the word *amulet*, from Latin *amuletum*, dates to the first century BCE. It comes from the verb *amoliri*, meaning "to drive away" or "to protect," and was typically used to describe small, portable objects often carried or worn on the body, especially around the neck. The word *talisman* derives from the Arabic word *tilsam*—an object that bears sacred symbols or signs containing magical power, especially for protection. The word *tilsam* actually comes from the Greek word *telesma*, which has myriad meanings, including "religious ceremony" and "ghost."[65] In the Middle East, "Arabic words such as *hijab*, *tilsam* (or *tilasam*), and *al-kitab* (literally 'writing' or 'book') were used to refer to Islamic textual amulets."[66]

Amulets are mainly objects used for protection, with the material used to craft the object being most significant. Talismans offer protection as well, but the ritual preparation often has more significance than the material used. In the crafting of talismans, knowing the names and the positions of the celestial bodies is of utmost importance, in addition to other factors that pertain to the ritual process, including words such as incantations and prayers, as well as other procedures used to consecrate the item. It is essential that a talisman be created at the precise time for its intended use. In ancient times, talismans (also referred to as *seals*) relied more on images and symbols than text; they were often associated with astrology and used to attract something (good luck) or repel something (like thieves, for example).[67] Additionally, the wearing of a talisman directly on the body wasn't a requirement.[68] Today we often use these words interchangeably, but noting their subtle difference is important.

In Middle Latin, the word *brevia*, meaning "brevet" or "brief text," was used for magical text that was written on parchment and could be worn or car-

---

64. Davies, *Grimoires.*

65. Lecouteux, *High Magic of Talismans.*

66. Skemer, *Binding Words*, 29.

67. Lecouteux, *High Magic of Talismans.*

68. Skemer, *Binding Words*, 8.

ried, sometimes accompanied by other objects, making it a type of amulet.[69] We sometimes see the word *charm* ("song" or "magic spell") used in conjunction with amulets. *Charm* sometimes refers to a textual amulet but not necessarily an object. Charms were most often acts of speech used for good or ill but could be written, just as textual amulets could also be spoken; charms could also contain instructions for specific ritual actions to be performed.

It seems as though writing was more often used for protective spells, and speaking was often used for healing: speech directed at the sick person, for example. When plant materials were used, it is noted that the manner of their collection or harvest was to be considered, and for written spells, the time of day was important.[70] There is also evidence that rhythmic meter was used.[71] Speaking the words of amuletic texts had many benefits. The "rhyme, repetition, and alliteration of charms produced a sonorous effect that appealed to users and had psychological effects."[72] Not only did rhythmic language aid the practitioner in recitation; words that sounded mystical or strange to the client would add to the belief in the spell's efficacy.

Even an illiterate person could use written magic—it didn't matter if the person understood or knew what the words meant. In fact, sometimes the "words" were just nonsense made up to appear mysterious. Even the person preparing the item didn't need to understand the incantations and secret names being used; what mattered was the belief that the spirits would understand.[73]

Amulets: The Most Popular Form of Written Magic

While charms, herbs, and other remedies were mostly used to cure existing illness, amulets were typically used as a means of prevention. Amulets worked through proximity—being worn or carried—as opposed to an ointment

---

69. Lecouteux, *High Magic of Talismans.*

70. Claude Lecouteux, *Traditional Magic Spells for Protection and Healing,* trans. Jon E. Graham (Rochester, VT: Inner Traditions, 2017), Kindle.

71. Christopher A. Faraone, "The Agonistic Context of Early Greek Binding Spells" in *Magika Hiera: Ancient Greek Magic and Religion,* ed. Christopher A. Faraone and Dirk Obbink (New York: Oxford University Press, 1991), 116.

72. Skemer, *Binding Words,* 153.

73. John G. Gager, *Curse Tablets and Binding Spells from the Ancient World* (New York: Oxford University Press, 1992), 10.

applied to the body or something ingested. But, again, there is overlap—one could anoint the body as a means of protection.[74]

In the case of amulets, the "process of scratching, drawing, or incising letters and other signs could transform a simple item into a magical artifact."[75] Small plates of metal referred to as "laminas" could be worn or carried and served a variety of purposes, such as healing or fertility, and were typically inscribed with a variety of symbols, letters, and even numbers.[76] Spells could also be inscribed on a container, such as a bowl or cup. But even just a word or phrase could serve as an amulet, and these textual amulets, using parchment, papyrus, wax discs, or paper could be folded, rolled, or both and be carried, worn on a specific area of the body, or spoken and then worn or carried. They could also be hidden in jewelry or worn in a leather pouch.

Greek papyrus amulets have been found in varying sizes (rectangular pieces or strips and other shapes), which were often rolled, then folded and tied. Writing could also appear on parchment, wooden tablets, sheets or disks of metal, and rings. There is evidence that "Arabic textual amulets were folded up or rolled (or both), then placed in suspension capsules worn horizontally"; they may have also been contained in "sacks, purses, and other containers suspended from the neck, attached to turbans, worn on belts, slung over the shoulder" or attached on the body in some other manner.[77]

Unsurprisingly, amulets were one of the most popular forms of magic in ancient Egypt, and a great deal of evidence survives. A popular type of amulet consisted of rolled papyri tied with string and placed into either leather pouches or metal tubes that could be worn on a cord or chain around the neck, and there were different types of amulets for the living and the dead.[78] Due to the "intimate relationship between images and words inherent in the hieroglyphic system of writing, an amulet could render a verbal wish into an object that could be worn."[79]

---

74. Kieckhefer, *Magic in the Middle Ages.*

75. Wilburn, *Materia Magica*, 65–66.

76. Kieckhefer, *Magic in the Middle Ages.*

77. Skemer, *Binding Words*, 28–29.

78. Bob Brier, *The History of Ancient Egypt* (Chantilly, VA: The Great Courses, 1999) 103; Skemer, *Binding Words*, 27.

79. *The Egyptian Book of the Dead*, 156.

Textual amulets could be "read, performed, displayed, visualized, and used interactively"; sometimes numerology was incorporated, pertaining to the number of times to fold the parchment, for example.[80] Some amulets, referred to as *narrative charms*, contained the story of a legendary or historical figure who had suffered in a similar way and was healed as an analogy to relieve illness.[81] Text could even be written directly on the body or ingested. In fact, some items used for edible spells include bread, butter, cheese, and fruits (see chapter 15). Monks and clerics would even inscribe communion wafers.[82] Ingesting holy writing was typically for the purpose of healing illnesses. In parts of Europe during the Middle Ages, "sacred words were written on bread or cheese to be swallowed by the sick," and there is evidence that manuscripts were washed or soaked with water so the ink could be consumed, and words on parchment could also be scraped into a drink. [83]

Curse Tablets

Particular types of amulets referred to as *curse tablets* have been found in ancient Greece, and the practice seems to have spread throughout the Roman Empire and into Britain. These are a specific type of amulet that was deposited into a well or spring or sometimes buried, rather than being worn. Typically, they were used to curse someone or request punishment or revenge for a wrongdoing, and they are believed to have been used by people of all social classes. However, the method was more complicated than just inscribing metal and depositing it. The whole process was nearly a type of business transaction, often involving "invocations, purifications, fumigations, prayers, instruments, rituals, and more."[84]

These curse tablets contained words inscribed on metal—sometimes thin sheets of lead or pewter called *lamellae*—and have long been of interest to researchers. In Greek, these spells inscribed on metal strips are often called *katadesmos*, from the verb *katadein*, which means "to bind up" or "to tie down."

---

80. Skemer, *Binding Words*, 127; 143.

81. Skemer, *Binding Words*, 105.

82. Lecouteux, *Dictionary of Ancient Magic Words and Spells*.

83. Davies, *Grimoires*; Kieckhefer, *Magic in the Middle Ages*.

84. Gager, *Curse Tablets and Binding Spells*, 18, 20.

Sometimes the Latin word *defixio* is used, or *defigere* ("to fasten" or "to nail down"). When *defixio* is used, it seems more specifically to describe pieces that were fastened closed with a nail.[85] But for consistency, I'll just refer to these types of amulets as curse tablets.

Some scholars believe these amulets were primarily verbal curses, but others believe that both the "spoken formula and the attendant gesture (i.e., the distortion of lead, wax, or some other pliable material) developed simultaneously."[86] The curse could be recited over the tablet while it was being prepared. One of the most significant deposits of these curse tablets was found at the Roman Baths in England, a place of public bathing with a temple built sometime between 60 and 70 CE. The baths were in use for several hundred years, and the museum there today is filled with artifacts from the area, including curse tablets.

Approximately 130 curse tablets have been discovered that were thrown into the spring, along with other offerings to the goddess Sulis Minerva, a syncretization of Sulis and Minerva (Roman goddess of wisdom). The exact meaning of *Sulis* isn't certain, but some scholars believe it may be associated with sight or the sun; she was the primary deity of this location. Before the Roman temple was built, some archaeologists speculate that the natural hot spring may have been used by the Celts for its perceived healing powers.

The words on the curse tablets typically mention items that were stolen and ask for the recovery of the property, punishment for the thief, or both. Some of the items described on the tablets include a hooded cloak, silver coins (in varying numbers), a bracelet, part of a plough, a blanket, a pair of gloves, a bronze vessel, and theft from a home (item stolen not specified). One of them says the thief should lose his mind and his eyes.[87] The curses sometimes contain a message to the goddess, asking for her help in recovering what was stolen. When the person creating the curse tablet knew (or thought they knew) the name or names of the culprits, those were also listed. Additionally, items such as plates, jugs, jewelry, candlesticks, and other personal belongings were left in the spring as offerings to Sulis Minerva.

---

85. *A History of Magic, Witchcraft and the Occult*, 34–35; Gager, *Curse Tablets and Binding Spells*, 30.

86. Faraone, "The Agonistic Context of Early Greek Binding Spells," 4.

87. Roman Baths, "Roman Curse Tablets," Bath, Somerset, November 2, 2018.

The curse tablets are fascinating to see, and it's certainly worth a visit to tour the baths if you can get there. You can even taste the water—the pump room offers water safe for drinking!

The small sheets of metal, which were once rolled or folded, have been "opened" so the markings are visible. There is one very special tablet on display that contains "the only words in British Celtic known to survive anywhere. The letters are from the Latin alphabet, but cannot be translated."[88]

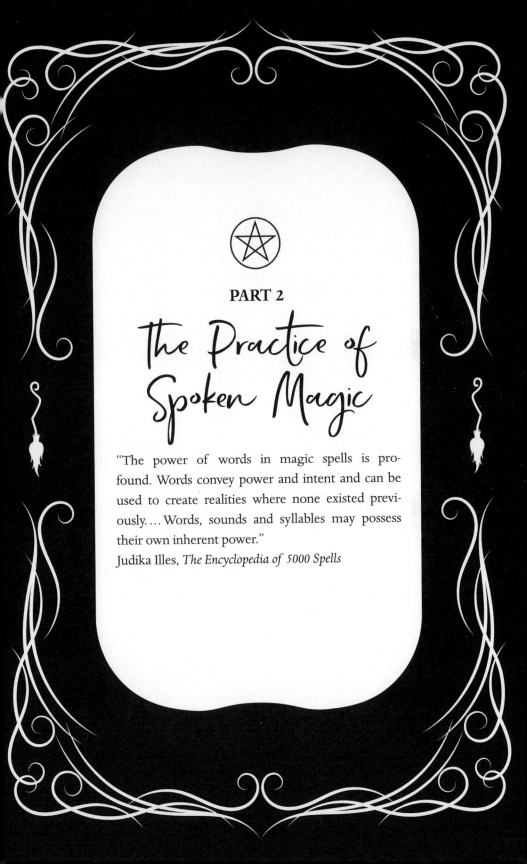

PART 2

The Practice of Spoken Magic

"The power of words in magic spells is profound. Words convey power and intent and can be used to create realities where none existed previously. ... Words, sounds and syllables may possess their own inherent power."

Judika Illes, *The Encyclopedia of 5000 Spells*

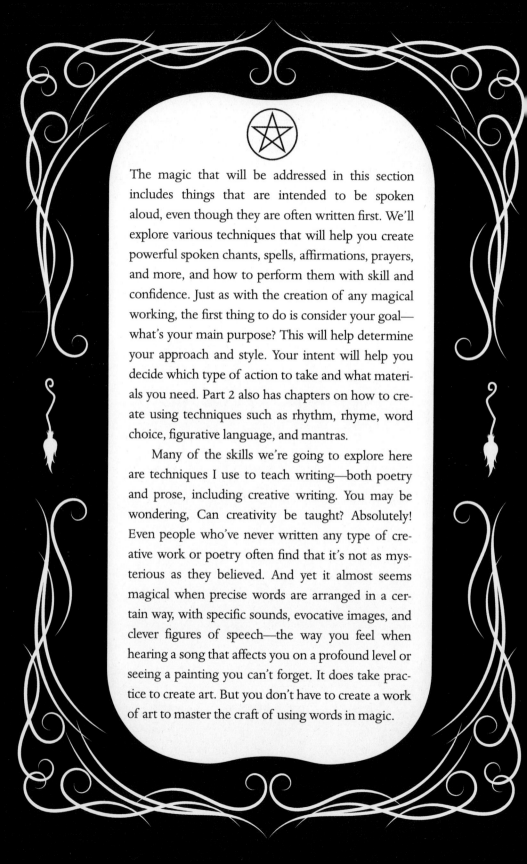

The magic that will be addressed in this section includes things that are intended to be spoken aloud, even though they are often written first. We'll explore various techniques that will help you create powerful spoken chants, spells, affirmations, prayers, and more, and how to perform them with skill and confidence. Just as with the creation of any magical working, the first thing to do is consider your goal—what's your main purpose? This will help determine your approach and style. Your intent will help you decide which type of action to take and what materials you need. Part 2 also has chapters on how to create using techniques such as rhythm, rhyme, word choice, figurative language, and mantras.

Many of the skills we're going to explore here are techniques I use to teach writing—both poetry and prose, including creative writing. You may be wondering, Can creativity be taught? Absolutely! Even people who've never written any type of creative work or poetry often find that it's not as mysterious as they believed. And yet it almost seems magical when precise words are arranged in a certain way, with specific sounds, evocative images, and clever figures of speech—the way you feel when hearing a song that affects you on a profound level or seeing a painting you can't forget. It does take practice to create art. But you don't have to create a work of art to master the craft of using words in magic.

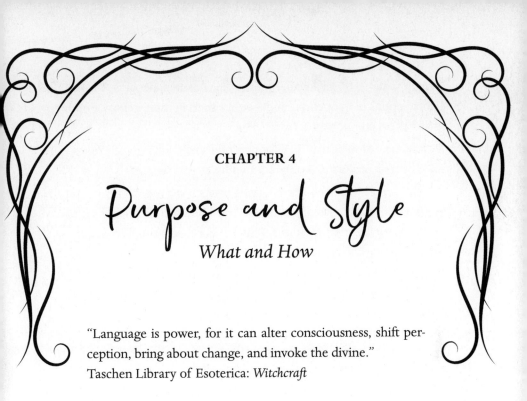

CHAPTER 4

Purpose and Style

What and How

"Language is power, for it can alter consciousness, shift perception, bring about change, and invoke the divine."
Taschen Library of Esoterica: *Witchcraft*

Before we begin the detailed discussion of words and techniques, let's break down some of the basic things for which we use words in magic. There is some overlap between many of these forms. This chapter will examine each of these in detail with examples.

What Is It? Prayer or Blessing, Spell or Affirmation?

While there is room for some overlap between these categories, here are basic definitions:

- *Prayer*: Requesting assistance from a deity or other power; also used in praise or to give thanks.
- *Blessing*: Wishes for goodwill or favor upon a person (or object); sometimes used in conjunction with prayer.
- *Spell*: A statement of something you want or desire; intent supported by visualization; often includes a spoken or written component and may include the use of specific actions, ingredients, or tools. Spells can be

simple actions; they can be written, sung, chanted, or silent.[89] An adjuration (serious oath or command) could also fit in this category, but often has a ritual component.

- *Affirmation*: Similar to a spell (or part of a spell), but typically just a spoken or written personal statement with a specific goal.

- *Ritual*: An act to celebrate something (event) or honor someone (person or deity). A ritual typically consists of symbolic action and may include prayers, spells, or affirmations. Raising energy in a ritual often involves chanting words or phrases.

- *Invocation/Evocation/Devocation*: These are all a type of communication, but each one has particular characteristics. They're usually statements that invite or dismiss the presence of deity.

In magical practice, spells usually have a specific goal, whereas a prayer or blessing doesn't necessarily have the same narrowly focused outcome. Historically, in some cultures, priests served as intermediaries, while a magician was the agent of change, and yet in some cultures, no distinction was made between these roles. Much has changed, and in many modern spiritual practices, the notion of an intermediary has become outdated. One simply prays to the deity of their choice. In *Magic in the Middle Ages*, Richard Kieckhefer offers these explanations: prayers are requests made to a specific deity; blessings are wishes addressed to someone in need; adjurations (and exorcisms) are commands aimed at an illness or other agent of disruption (adjurations are what we typically call spells). Basically, prayers and blessings can be used with magic but are not themselves inherently magical. He goes on to mention a fourth type, less common, the "incantations articulating the meaning of sympathetic magic."[90] This means that words would be spoken that explain the reason behind a particular action or use of a specific item.

Let's use the celebration of Imbolc as an example to illustrate the variety of purposes and techniques. There are multiple things you could do:

---

89. Chanting is both a method of speaking and a noun—a "chant" can be a word, phrase, or even just sounds. I will make the distinction clear each time I use the word.

90. Kieckhefer, *Magic in the Middle Ages*.

- write a prayer that honors or praises the goddess Brigit; purpose: celebrate her traits
- pray "to" Brigit; purpose: to ask for something
- invoke or evoke Brigit; purpose: invite her into your celebration, call her attention, or invite her spirit inside you
- create a spell to cast in the spirit of the holiday for a variety of purposes: renewal, creativity, etc.
- create a ritual to be performed that contains all of these aspects or just celebrates the traits of the sabbat

Each of these presents an occasion for words—written or spoken. To begin, let your purpose guide you. Once you know the *why*, then focus on the *how*. For example, if you're performing a solitary ritual to celebrate, you wouldn't need a complex narrative that contains parts for several speakers. If your purpose is to simply honor the season, you could write a poem (and say it aloud) or sing a song. If you're speaking directly "to" Brigit, a prayer would be appropriate. If you're casting a spell for a specific outcome, you could chant it or write something as part of the spell and take action in a ritual. You could also create an affirmation. Yes, there is overlap here. Try not to overthink it.

Let's look at an example of each type.

Prayers and Blessings

Using Imbolc as an example, here's a piece I wrote many years ago.[91]

> *Warm me, Brigit, light the fire,*
> *within and without.*
> *In transformation and desire,*
> *extinguish all my doubt.*
> *Teach me, Brigit, light the flame,*
> *my passions burning higher,*

---

91. Most of the examples used in this book are my own. I believe in using my own work to demonstrate the techniques because I can provide an analysis of my thought process and strategy without guessing at the intent of something written by someone else; Ember Grant, *Magical Candle Crafting: Create Your Own Candles for Spells & Rituals* (Woodbury, MN: Llewellyn Publications, 2011), 97

creative spark I seek to claim—
let me be inspired.
Heal me, Brigit, hearth ignite,
help me know the way.
Guide me with your sacred light,
with me always stay.

This piece was titled a "chant" in my first book (*Magical Candle Crafting*). However, it's more accurately (in its function and purpose) a prayer. Note that it addresses Brigit directly and asks for things like guidance, healing, and inspiration. (Yes, those are spell traits too.) This piece could be accompanied with actions and objects to reinforce the goal, but note that there are several "goals" here: extinguish doubt (about what?), passion, creativity, inspiration, guidance; it's a little too "busy" to be a spell.

Here's another example of a prayer:

To Gaia, Mother Earth,
Mother of us all—
nurture those in need, the homeless
and the hungry, help them find
the sustenance they need.
Also guide the hands and hearts
of those who are able
to give when they can,
to help make change
in the world.
Blessed Be.

These two prayers have some essential things in common: (1) a deity is being addressed and (2) something specific is being requested. Notice that the first prayer has a much more rhythmic and musical style, using rhyme, for example, while the second one doesn't contain those features. But these prayers also contain differences. In the first one, the speaker is asking for something; in the second one, the speaker is requesting help for others.

When writing a prayer, the first thing to consider is to whom you are speaking. Are you addressing a deity? Next, what are you praying for? Are you asking for something in particular? Is it for yourself or someone else? Is it just a general hymn of praise or one of devotion or thanks? All these are important aspects.[92] Think of prayer as a conversation. After you've spoken the words, be sure to sit for a while in contemplation and reflection. It may be helpful if you think of a prayer as a letter that contains "an address, a greeting, a main body, and a closing."[93] The second of these two examples contains these components, but the first one does not. That doesn't mean one is better or one is incorrect; they're just different styles. But both contain the name of the deity being addressed and a specific request or plea.

Blessings, in most cases, are not as specific as a prayer, so deity need not be addressed. Blessings are often used for people or objects. Here's a very simple blessing I created for my Yule tree. First, I considered what was most important: I wanted to honor the tree and give thanks for it. I also wanted to initiate it as a symbol for the season and perhaps charge it with positive energy for the year ahead. I could just say those things, but I wanted something more formal and ceremonial.

Yuletide Tree Blessing

We are thankful for this tree,
a symbol as in days of old,
to cheer us and be ever-green
while land is bare and air is cold.

Let every branch and point of light
and ornament that glows,
bring a year filled with delight
and yuletide cheer that grows.

Again, notice the features of this blessing. It expresses thanks and also asks for the object to "do" something—to bring cheer.

---

92. A hymn is technically a prayer that is sung, and they don't usually make a specific request.

93. Elizabeth Barrette, *Composing Magic: How to Create Magical Spells, Rituals, Blessings, Chants, and Prayers* (Franklin Lakes, NJ: New Page Books, 2007), Kindle.

Spells and Affirmations

To continue using Imbolc as an example, the previous prayer to Brigit could be revised to create a spell specifically for one goal (with or without using Brigit's name) by tightening the focus to make it more precise. Note here that I've changed the words to ask for "creative power." This is more specific and doesn't include the line about healing. This is a spell for inspiration.

Brigit, help me be inspired,

guide me with your light.

Creative power flows through me

with every word I write.

Of course, this spell would most likely be accompanied by visualization techniques or the use of specific items such as crystals, herbs, or candles. Addressing a deity is optional and is usually determined by personal preference.

To use this same piece as an affirmation, the words could be spoken as a simple statement. Typically, affirmations are short statements that can be easily memorized and repeated, or written and placed where they can be seen. They are often part of a spell. This single line of the spell could be an affirmation:

Creative power flows through me with every word I write.

Note that in both examples the phrase is in present tense—the statement doesn't ask for the power "to flow" or say that it "will flow." It states that it currently "flows." It's already happening. This can aid with visualization. You're not hoping something will happen; you know that it's happening now. Instead of "will be," say, "is." For example, instead of "As I drink this tea, every bit of illness in my body will be cured, will be banished, will be healed," say, "As I drink this tea, every bit of illness in my body *is* cured, *is* banished, *is* healed." Or, simply, "I am healed."

A spell can have many components or be quite simple, but even simple spells should undergo a period of planning in order to take advantage of all the various aspects involved. Spells typically contain words, actions, and materials (tools, candles, etc.), but they don't have to include all these things. However, everything should be considered during the planning process to ensure success. (See chapter 21.)

Rituals

Now we'll briefly explore how ritual differs from prayer, blessing, spell, and affirmation. In addition, we'll explore how to write invocations, evocations, devocations, and quarter calls, which are commonly part of a ritual.

A ritual is typically ceremonial and involves specific actions performed in a certain order; these actions can be performed for celebration or to raise energy for a specific purpose. Rituals can be performed in groups or alone and are usually a bit more formal than a spell. Prayers, blessings, spells, and affirmations can all be part of a ritual. One thing that sets a ritual apart is the symbolic action that takes place. Just like with a spell or prayer, a ritual must have a specific purpose.

Basic parts of a ritual include multiple actions (see chapter 21 for a ritual template):

- creating sacred space / opening (calling quarters, stating intent), inviting divinity: invocation / evocation
- main action, raising energy, release
- communion / cakes and ale / libations / offering
- devocation / closing the circle

Writing a complete ritual involves not only creating the various parts that are spoken but designing all the actions, decorations, etc. For now, let's just look at a few of the things spoken in a ritual: quarter calls and an invocation.

Quarter Calls

Just like every other aspect of magic, quarter calls can be elaborate or very simple. Basically, you're addressing the four directions or the Elements (or both) and inviting them into your circle. The purpose and function vary from formal ceremonial magic to a more relaxed atmosphere and are, like everything else, personal choice.

A simple quarter call can just address each direction or Element and say "Hail and welcome." But if you'd like to be more specific, here's an example. Notice how this one addresses the particular characteristics and qualities of each Element:

I greet the North
and honor the Element of Earth.
Soil and sand that I call home,
field and flower, tree and stone.
May the Earth nourish me.
  Hail and welcome!

I greet the East
and honor the Element of Air.
Changing winds, air to breathe,
precious atmosphere and breeze.
May the Air inspire me.
  Hail and welcome!

I greet the South
and honor the Element of Fire.
Energy of sun so bright,
warmth and heat, radiant light.
May the Fire excite me.
  Hail and welcome!

I greet the West
and honor the Element of Water.
Drink of life in flow or freeze,
rain and river, spring and sea.
May the Water renew me.
  Hail and welcome!

There is a pattern here that is repeated for each Element, beginning with addressing the purpose of the ritual, stating the power of each Element, and requesting that its qualities be present and/or affect the speaker. (Pattern and repetition will be discussed further in chapters 5 and 6.)

Invocations, Evocations, and Devocations

Invocation and evocation are similar in many ways, in that they are invitations to an entity of some kind to enter your sacred space. Both of these acts call attention to something and encourage participation. Invocation is also the act of summoning something or someone for aid or guidance, especially asking for the entity to be felt fully in the mind and body of the practitioner. Think of the "i" in the word *invocation* as a personal "invitation" to an entity. The word *evocation* technically means the act of bringing or recalling a feeling, memory, or image to the conscious mind. In magical practice, it is used to call an entity into an object or simply ask for the presence of the entity in a larger ritual space, as opposed to a personal interaction. Think of the difference this way: invocation is the summoning of powers into the self from a divine source; evocation is used for calling upon lesser spirits or arousing specific feelings or emotions. Grammatically speaking, invoking is active and direct, while evoking is passive and indirect, often associated with emotions. In a nonmagical setting, we "invoke" a law or authority figure or precedent; we "evoke" feelings or bring to mind a past emotion or memory; it can also be used for making things happen: "evoking" a strong response. Most modern practitioners of Western magic use them this way: invoking is to invite a spirit to enter your body; evoking is calling upon a spirit or deity to join in a ritual, to simply be present. Just as with prayer, invocations and evocations should be specific, naming and describing the characteristics of the entity. They can take any form you wish—rhymed or unrhymed, long and detailed or short and simple. In a ritual setting, the invocation or evocation should also mention the specific intent and purpose. It should go without saying that the attitude should be one of respect and include a "thank you" to the entity for its presence. In fact, that's one of the reasons for a devocation.

Devocation is to send away or call off, typically after invoking or evoking. Rather than thinking of it as a dismissal, consider it a farewell. This act brings closure to the experience as well as expressing thanks and being sure that whatever entity is invoked or evoked is appropriately and respectfully returned to its proper place.

Let's use Brigit as an example once again.

Invocation:

Goddess Brigit, threefold mistress of the hearth, poetry, and smithcraft,
kindly hear my call. Fill me, body, mind, and soul
with your healing light, your creative inspiration, and your strength.

Devocation:

Brigit, I have felt your energy in my body, mind, and soul.
Thank you for your healing light, your creative inspiration, and your strength.
Return now to your dwelling place with my deepest gratitude. Hail and farewell!

Evocation:

Goddess Brigit, threefold mistress of the hearth, poetry, and smithcraft,
kindly hear our call. Join our ritual circle, enter our sacred space, be with us
and share your healing light, your creative inspiration, and your strength.

Devocation:

Goddess Brigit, we have felt your presence in this sacred space.
You have honored us, and we are deeply thankful.
Return now to your dwelling place with our sincerest gratitude. Hail and farewell!

Note that these can be adapted for solitary or group activities. Also notice the similarity of language between the invocation and devocation and the use of repetition. Again, this helps keep the purpose and focus in mind and also creates a sense of balance.

After speaking the words of invocation or evocation, you may wish to chant a few lines or words while visualizing the process. For example, during invocation in this case, you could repeat the words "Fill me, body, mind, and soul" over and over while visualizing Brigit's presence entering you and granting you the gifts you mentioned.

What about Poetry?

You might be wondering if these written pieces can be considered poems. In poetry, *how* something is being said is as important as *what* is being said. A poem can be a spell and a spell can be a poem, but just keep in mind they can be quite different. In my practice, they are usually separate things. I sometimes write poems to use in rituals, but if I want words to chant during a spell or if I'm creating a group ritual that contains words that people will need to chant together, I approach it in a very different way than I do my poetry.

While precise words are important in each of these formats, spells typically need to function on a different level than poems. They do share many traits, but one main difference is purpose and goal. I don't always have those in mind when I write a poem. Sometimes poems are expressions of feelings or a description that moves me; I'm not asking for something or raising energy like I would in a spell. But the skills are transferable. Knowing when and how to use each approach is the key. Chapter 19 explores some forms of formal poetic verse you can try.

In *The Spiral Dance*, Starhawk reminds us that "Witchcraft has always been a religion of poetry, not theology."[94] This is a perfect metaphor for how we understand things beyond words. That may seem counterintuitive to the point of this book, but it's not. Working magic is about connecting and transcending; it's about our emotions, senses—things that we typically can't describe using words. This statement reminds us that poetry, like magic, is a way of understanding our world that goes beyond words. Poetry, like magic, works on a different level than our normal awareness.

Starhawk makes another significant point about the role of language in magic—how not just words but symbols and images all work together to affect our levels of consciousness and awareness. Words uttered in an altered state of consciousness can create change. She says, "poetry, itself a form of magic, is magic speech."[95] There is certainly a place for poetry in the practice of magic.

Bottom line: your words should serve your purpose completely. Whatever style you choose, be precise and true to your goal. The words should project your intent. You are speaking (or writing) something into existence.

---

94. Starhawk, *The Spiral Dance: A Rebirth of the Ancient Religion of the Great Goddess*, 20th anniversary edition (San Francisco: Harper, 1999), 32.

95. Starhawk, *The Spiral Dance*, 137.

Word-Witch Practice
Purpose and Style

Try these activities to practice using the various styles and approaches discussed in this chapter.

- Choose an event, deity, or desired goal and practice writing an appropriate prayer, blessing, affirmation, spell, quarter calls, and invocation or evocation. Follow the examples to distinguish between the purposes of each piece. Refer to the checklists for creating and the ritual template in chapter 21 as needed.

- If you already write poetry, consider to what extent your poems can be used in your magical practice.

- Make lists of words that describe specific feelings and emotions that you'd like to evoke during prayer or ritual. Try to go beyond obvious words like *devotion, peace, love,* etc.

CHAPTER 5

Chanting, Part 1

Rhyme

"All existence is simply an arrangement of silence and sound."
Om Swami, *The Ancient Science of Mantras*

Many years ago, I wrote an article for *Llewellyn's Magical Almanac* called "The Three R's of Chant Writing: Rhyme, Rhythm, and Repetition."[96] I have written literally hundreds of spells—everything from simple affirmations to elaborate group rituals—and I almost always use rhyme and rhythm if the words are meant to be chanted. In the next two chapters, we'll explore these techniques in detail and other ways to create musical sounds with words. But before we go any further, let's take a moment to actually define the word *chant*—both as a noun and a verb.

Chanting

Magic words have been used throughout history for everything from safe travel to cursing others. But one thing seems to be common: spells were typically created using "meter and rhyme—making them easy to chant."[97] A *chant* is a word

---

96. Ember Grant, "The Three R's of Chant Writing: Rhyme, Rhythm, and Repetition," *Llewellyn's 2012 Magical Almanac* (Llewellyn Worldwide: Woodbury, 2011), 26–33.

97. *A History of Magic, Witchcraft and the Occult*, 92.

or phrase, typically rhythmic in nature, that is spoken in unison by a group of people; it also means to say or shout something repeatedly—a simple song or short phrase. The technique can be used in everything from prayer to sporting events. When we refer to a "chant" as a thing, we're referring to the set of words being repeated. That's the essence of chanting—repetition. The simplest definition of chanting is to speak or sing a word or phrase over and over.

Chanting is a good choice for affirmations, invocations, prayers, and raising energy. Use chanting when you want to repeat something over and over again easily—to be simple and direct. Chants can also be part of a longer recitation, such as a refrain or a line or two at the end of a long prayer or affirmation. Many of the components we're exploring here will help you write spells, invocations, and prayers that are easy to remember and recite.

Types of Rhyme

Rhyme is easy; it comes to us almost without effort. Rhyme not only serves the function of helping us remember the lines for memorization; it's one of the easiest ways to create a musical effect. One reason for rhyme's appeal is that humans love patterns, and we often expect to hear a similar sound repeated. However, rhyming (especially end rhymes at the ends of lines) has been accused of having a "singsong" quality that many people associate with something too simple to be good poetry. That's because so many rhymes are overused and clichéd. In spell writing, however, I would argue that this doesn't matter. You really can't go wrong with classic rhyming words as long as they are meaningful to you. But if you find the rhymes boring or distracting, or you want to be more inventive, there are many other approaches you can take.

One benefit of rhyming is that it makes the words easier to memorize, and memorization is good for your brain. While today it may be regarded as having little value in education, memorization does still have its merits. There is a link between memorization and the development of critical thinking skills.[98] Magically speaking, when you've memorized the words to an affirmation or prayer, you can focus more fully on your intent.

---

98. Natalie Wexler, "Why Memorizing Stuff Can Be Good for You," Forbes, April 29, 2019, https://www
    .forbes.com/sites/nataliewexler/2019/04/29/why-memorizing-stuff-can-be-good-for-you/.

I'll be using lots of poetic terminology in this book, so let's look at how we define the various types of rhyming words:

- A *pure* or *perfect rhyme* is the simplest and easiest: *believe* and *relieve*, for example, or *fire* and *desire*. This is also the kind of rhyme that can quickly become boring or clichéd. Still, for spells, affirmations, prayers, or invocations that are easy to memorize and chant, don't discount the value of simplicity. *Identical rhyme* is just using the same word twice.

- A *slant rhyme* or *off-rhyme* (also called *near rhyme* or *half rhyme*) is a rhyme that's close but not exact. This can be achieved by using words that look like they could rhyme but don't, or by using sounds that almost sound the same. Words like *chart, dark, park,* and *cart,* or *world, word,* and *sword.*

- *Apocopated* or *"cut-off" rhyme* is the term used when the last syllable of one of the rhyming words is missing: *snap* and *happen,* or *mat* and *flatter.*

- *Eye rhyme* is when two words look like they should rhyme but don't: *dough* and *cough.*

These next terms are not about the actual words, but concern their place-ment in a written verse:[99]

- *End rhyme* is the most common type of rhyme; the words used in this type of rhyme appear at the ends of lines in a stanza.[100]

- *Internal rhymes* are rhyming words that occur in the middle of a line instead of (or in addition to) at the ends or across several different lines.

Another poetic term is *rhyme scheme*. This is how we describe specific rhym-ing patterns at the ends of lines. We use the letters of the alphabet to designate the words that sound alike in order to keep track of the pattern, especially in longer pieces or types of poetry that require a rhyming formula (see chapter 19). Rhyme schemes are fun—you can alternate between the end rhymes, repeat them in a specific order, or have only every other line rhyme. Here are some popular end-rhyme schemes:

---

99. Remember, even though some of these techniques pertain to the act of writing printed pieces, the end goal with the piece you're creating (in this context) is to speak out loud the words you've written.

100. A *stanza* is a set of lines grouped together and separated by a space.

- Couplets are pairs of lines in a row: aa bb cc.

Twinkle, twinkle, little star	*a*
how I wonder what you are	*a*
up above the world so high	*b*
like a diamond in the sky	*b*

- A *tercet* or *triplet* is a series of three, like this: aaa bbb ccc ddd; *terza rima* is a similar concept: aba bcb cdc ded.

- The *quatrain* is a set of four lines that have alternating rhymes, for example: abab cdcd.

There are many more variations and specific forms of poems, like sonnets, that display a very specific rhyme scheme (see chapter 19).

A few words in defense of the end rhyme: when done well, with a subtle touch, it avoids a singsong quality. Here's another example from my own work. This is from *The Book of Crystal Spells*.[101]

Spell for Unity and Wholeness

All I am and will become	1
is in my reach, it is the sum	2
of all I am and all I've done;	3
what I wish, I will become.	4
Part of whole and every part	5
is in my body, soul, and heart,	6
with the cosmos I am one—	7
by earth and sky, by moon and sun.	8

This piece uses lots of end rhymes, but notice how lines one and two don't have punctuation? You're forced to keep going to the next lines to complete the statement. Those lines are *enjambed* (this means you're forced to keep reading to complete the thought), and this is one way to play with rhyme so that the end rhymes don't always draw all the attention. When you hear the words spoken aloud, the sounds still create a musical effect. The same thing happens

---

101. I revised the second to last line of this piece. The original version was "with the universe I'm one—" I changed it to achieve a more even rhythm; Ember Grant, *The Book of Crystal Spells: Magical Uses for Stones, Crystals, Minerals … and Even Sand* (Woodbury, MN: Llewellyn Publications, 2013), 107.

with line five. *End-stopped lines* are complete thoughts on their own, such as line seven. End-stopped lines usually use some type of punctuation (but not always). Poetically speaking, sentences and lines are not the same thing.

Here's another example of how to arrange lines. This is from *The Second Book of Crystal Spells*.[102]

A Spell to Release Worry

Upon me worry has no hold; I am here, let time unfold.
Never waste a single minute; don't forget that I am in it
for as long as time allows—I repeat these earnest vows.
Wasted time can't be recovered; I am willing to discover
all I know that waits for me—for good of all so shall it be.

Here's the same piece with shorter lines. That changes the rhyme from internal to end rhyme. This difference is really only obvious if the verse is written. When it's spoken, there isn't much change.

Upon me worry has no hold;
I am here, let time unfold.
Never waste a single minute;
don't forget that I am in it
for as long as time allows—
I repeat these earnest vows.
Wasted time can't be recovered;
I am willing to discover
all I know that waits for me—
for good of all so shall it be.

The main thing I want to point out here is the use of enjambment. In both examples, this can be seen after the words "I am in it" and "discover." Notice how you have to keep reading after these phrases. These lines are only lightly enjambed (as opposed to strongly enjambed). This means they could almost

---

102. Ember Grant, *The Second Book of Crystal Spells: More Magical Uses for Stones, Crystals, Minerals … Even Salt* (Woodbury, MN: Llewellyn Publications, 2016), 126–27.

stand alone. Getting creative with line breaks can help create rhythm while still using rhymes. (For more on line breaks, see chapter 9.)

Also, I want to point out the inversion of the words at the beginning: I say, "Upon me worry has no hold" instead of saying, "Worry has no hold on me," which sounds more modern and "normal." I would never use that inversion in a poem—it sounds archaic and outdated, and gives the impression of trying to "force" the rhythm and rhyme to fit.[103] But for a spell, I like it. I prefer the formal sound, and it creates the desired rhyme and rhythm.

Rhyme does serve another purpose beyond helping us remember and creating music—it can also reinforce the meanings of words and, ultimately, your entire piece of writing. The best use of rhyme preserves meaning and doesn't just rhyme for the sake of rhyming. Rhymed words stand out in a piece, so make them count. Make these words important, perhaps key words in your spell. Rhyme also produces a sense of echo, gives a feeling of closure, and satisfies expectation.[104]

You can capitalize on that feature in your spell or prayer by linking words together to reinforce your goal. Words like *desire, fire,* and *higher* all work together to create an image. And don't forget you can also rhyme the sounds of multiple words, like I did with "minute" and "I am in it."

In addition to rhyme, here are some more techniques to help create a pleasant combination of sounds:

- *Assonance* is the similar sound of vowels in words. Consider the words *ignite, higher, fire, desire,* and *my*—they all have a long "i" sound. The words *branch* and *enchant* have an "a" sound; *road* and *smoke* both have a long "o" sound.
- *Consonance* is the similar sound of consonants in a word. For example, the words *yellow, field,* and *while* all contain the "l" sound.

---

103. There's actually a name for this technique: *anastrophe*—the act of inverting the normal order of the parts of a sentence in order to draw emphasis or accommodate a particular rhythmic or rhyming pattern.

104. Kim Addonizio and Dorianne Laux, *The Poet's Companion: A Guide to the Pleasures of Writing Poetry* (New York: W. W. Norton and Co., 1997), 145.

- *Alliteration* is the repetition of a sound at the beginning of words—for example, *bright, Brigit, beautiful,* and *burning.* Consider how the combination of sounds can create a musical effect. For example, the phrase *languid yellow light* contains alliteration and consonance—the "l" sound. The words *flower* and *power* both have the "owr," so they rhyme and use assonance.

Word-Witch Practice
Rhyme

Here are some ways to experiment with rhyme and other sound combinations. Creative writers frequently use exercises and prompts like these to come up with new and interesting phrases and ideas; simple activities like this can generate beautiful, original compositions.

- Make a list of words with pure or perfect rhyme that you would consider using in a spell, affirmation, prayer, etc. One way to begin is to consider your goal—perhaps the name (or characteristics) of a deity, or the qualities of an Element (Earth, Air, Fire, Water). You could also consider other words you use often—for example, *moon, sun, wind, breeze, seed, grow, trees, stone, time, protect, heal,* etc., or phrases like *So mote it be* or *For the good of all.* After you've exhausted all the exact rhymes you can think of, refer to a rhyming dictionary (try RhymeZone.com) and see if you can find some new rhyming words, including those with more syllables than the original word. (For example, easy words that rhyme with *grow* are *snow, blow, go, below, though, flow, crow, doe, row, sew, slow.* Other examples that have multiple syllables are *borrow, although, hello, tempo, willow, indigo, manifesto,* etc.)

- Using the list you created using exact rhymes, look for slant rhymes or come up with words that create apocopated rhymes.

- Engage in some wordplay. Look for words that have assonance or consonance, write them down, and then add rhymes. For example, words such as *grow*, *evoke*, and *smoke*; *rain*, *flame*, and *tame*.
- Play with alliteration. Begin with a word and then list words that begin with the same first letter. Consult a dictionary if you wish.
- Choose a few words from any of these lists and use them as starting points to create spells and prayers.

CHAPTER 6

Chanting, Part 2

Rhythm

"Through rhythm…[we reunite ourselves] with the ecstasy and terror of a moving universe."
Nims and Mason, *Western Wind*

Rhythm, whether achieved by the sound of drums, dancing, or chanting, has long been integral to the magical experience—a basic way to reach altered states of consciousness. Using words, one essential aspect of phrases you intend to chant is the rhythm—the "beat" of the piece. In this chapter, we'll explore some basic ways to create rhythm in a spoken work. You don't need a detailed understanding of poetic meter; just considering the syllables is enough to create rhythm. As with using rhyme, I don't use this technique in every spell I write. However, when it's something that I know will be chanted, I always give careful consideration to this aspect of the piece; the arrangement of syllables does make a difference. Another technique you can use to create rhythm is the act of repetition.

Using Syllables to Create Rhythm

First, let's look at how to use syllables to create a pleasant rhythm. Continuing with my earlier example, here are the same lines, but changed to make the request without asking Brigit. The numbers refer to the number of syllables in each line.

Inspiration come to me,	7
keep me reaching higher.	6
Give me everything I need	7
for achieving my desire.	8

Upon saying these words out loud, do you notice how the rhythm in the last line feels "off"? That's because the last line has eight syllables; the previous lines alternate between six and seven syllables.

In the next example, I've made a change to the last line:

Inspiration come to me,	7
keep me reaching higher.	6
Give me everything I need,	7
grant me my desire.	6

The last line sounds better with six syllables instead of eight; the piece ends up with alternating lines of seven and six syllables, making it feel more even.

Here's another example:

Smoke that rises take away	7
negative energy—	6
these thoughts can't stay.	4
Anger, misery, worry, and doubt,	9
smoke please carry them	5
out, out, out!	3

While there's nothing wrong with this chant, here is a version that I revised for a more even rhythm:

Smoke that rises take away	7
what I don't need—	4
these thoughts can't stay.	4
Anger, misery, and doubt,	7
smoke please send them	4
out, out, out!	3

There's a stronger sense of rhythm here because of the syllabic pattern of seven and four. Also note the repetition of *out* at the end. This is a good example of when you'd use a forceful tone—perhaps even shout—and physically wave incense smoke out the window, visualizing negative energy going with it.

Here's another example. Each of these lines has five syllables (and five is a number of protection—see chapter 17, Words and Numbers):

let this amulet

serve me and protect

Notice how these lines don't have a pleasant rhythm—it feels uneven, even though each line has five syllables.[105] This is where an understanding of poetic meter can make a difference. *Meter* is the use of strategically placed stressed and unstressed syllables (see chapter 19).

let this **am** u let

serve me and pro **tect**

The bold text indicates where stress is located.

It's really not a science in most cases where the stress occurs, especially with one-syllable words. Words with multiple syllables can be checked in the dictionary, but that doesn't always indicate how the word feels and sounds in the verse. It's often up to the speaker or performer. Just like no two musicians will play or sing the same song in exactly the same way, despite notes on the page, there is a difference in performing or chanting an incantation, prayer, or spell (unless it's very simple with one-syllable words).

So I rearranged things:

let me **now** protect,

charge this **amulet**

These syllables are more evenly stressed, but I still don't like it. If I want to use the words "amulet" and "protect" together and preserve the slant rhyme, here's another way (the ˘ symbol represents an unstressed syllable; the - indicates a stressed syllable):

---

105. Chapter 9 contains a closer look at line breaks.

> To **guard** and **to** pro-*tect,*   ˘ _ ˘ _ ˘ _
>
> I **charge** this **am**-*u-let*   ˘ _ ˘ _ ˘ ˘

While "amulet" is a three-syllable word, and technically the first syllable has the stress, the last syllable can be given a bit more force if you'd like while you're chanting. But still, this gives a pattern at the beginning of each line with an unstressed syllable followed by a stressed one.

The one-syllable words are the tricky ones, since you can decide how much or how little to stress them, just as you can give the word "amulet" more cadence by emphasizing the last syllable a bit more than you normally would.

In this example, each line has six syllables (these lines could also be inverted). This arrangement also uses the parallel structure (more on that later) of "to" guard and "to" protect, which helps create a feeling of balance. The second syllable of each line is stressed: "guard" and "charge," and both words have the "a" sound. In addition, the words "protect" and "amulet" both end with the "t" sound. Scansion is more of an art than an actual science. But knowing how to do it can help if your arrangement of words feels "off" and you're not sure why.[106] (For more on this topic, see chapter 19.)

Here's another example. This is from a chant to use during water writing (see chapter 14):

> *Water, let this word I write*
>
> *conjure and fulfill my need;*
>
> *water, as I form this word*
>
> *I know my goal will succeed.*

Look closely at that last line. While it has seven syllables like the others, it doesn't have the same rhythmic beat as the other lines. The issue concerns the placement of stressed and unstressed syllables:

> **Water,** **let** this **word** I **write**   _ ˘ _ ˘ _ ˘ _
>
> **conjure** and **fulfill** my **need;**   _ ˘ _ ˘ _ ˘ _
>
> **water,** as I **form** this **word**   _ ˘ _ ˘ _ ˘ _
>
> *I know my goal will succeed.*

---

106. *Scansion* is the practice of locating the stressed and unstressed syllables in lines of poetry.

Saying the words naturally, it's like this: "I **know** my **goal** will suc**ceed**," but it doesn't sound right in the context of this verse. That's because the pattern of stressed and unstressed syllables is this: ˇ- ˇ- ˇ ˇ-

You could force the rhythm: "I know **my** goal **will** suc**ceed**," but it sounds awkward.

In this case, the words need to be changed to preserve the pattern of rhythm. This works better: "**let** this **mag**ic **spell** suc**ceed**." This change not only preserves the pattern of seven syllables per line, but it matches the pattern of stressed and unstressed syllables in the previous lines.

Also, when I first wrote this chant, line two was "manifest and fill my need," but I changed it to be more faithful to the rhythm since "manifest" has three syllables. It could have worked, but I decided "conjure" was the better choice, and then I used "fulfill" instead of "fill." Here's the final version:

Water, let this word I write
conjure and fulfill my need;
water, as I form this word
let this magic spell succeed.

Here's one more example, just to prove that having even syllables doesn't always mean the rhythm is better. The coven I was in many years ago often used this chant at springtime:

seed, sprout, stem, leaf, bud, flower[107]

I don't know the origin of this chant, but I always thought, Why not use the word "blossom" for alliteration with "bud"? And then I thought, Why not the word "bloom," which would also preserve the pattern of one-syllable words? But when I chant it, especially quickly to build energy, I like "flower" better. Maybe it's because of the "l" and "f" in both "flower" and "leaf." It all comes down to personal preference, what sounds and feels best to you. These techniques are just ways to experiment and help you achieve your desired result.

Obviously, using rhyme and rhythm in your magic isn't a requirement; I don't apply all these guidelines every time I write a chant. These are just options. If all this seems like overthinking to you, you can just speak your affirmation or

---

107. Greenwood Circle, chant, c. 2004–2008.

words to charge the object. You can simply say, "I charge this amulet for protection from all harm. So mote it be." There's nothing wrong with that. However, I do believe these skills and techniques can increase the creativity of your chant writing and lead to an even more effective magical practice.

Using Repetition to Create Rhythm

Repetition can create a sense of rhythm and has been employed by musicians and bards for thousands of years. Repeating something creates emphasis and focus. And like rhyme, it can also make a rhythmic sound and help you remember the words.

Refrains (the repetition of a word or phrase) are a perfect example of repetition put to good use, and they have a long history in prayers, hymns, invocations, and other spiritual practices. The following examples use refrain to reinforce meaning and create rhythm.

This chant could be part of a ritual that celebrates cycles and could be used to raise energy; the refrain of "waxing, waning" highlights the purpose.

Cycles of life, waxing, waning.

Success and strife, waxing, waning.

Tides of power, waxing, waning.

Seed to flower, waxing, waning.

Notice that this example also uses rhyme ("life" and "strife"; "power" and "flower"), and there is an even syllabic rhythm in lines one and two and lines three and four.

This next example is part of a cleansing spell to banish negativity; the "trouble me no more" refrain is the goal of the spell.

Unwanted presence now be gone,

trouble me no more.

I banish this unwelcome force,

trouble me no more.

Cause me no more pain,

go back from where you came,

trouble me no more.

The next example is from a spell to break bonds. The repetition of "release this bond" is a constant reminder of the spell's purpose and would be accompanied by the cutting of a rope or ribbon.

As the moon wanes,
Release this bond.
As the candle expires,
Release this bond.
As I cut the cord,
Release this bond.
I am free.

Repetition doesn't only involve refrains. You can repeat a single word, a phrase, an image, or create repeating patterns with the way lines and stanzas are organized. In the last example, "release this bond" is the goal of the spell, and it's repeated three times. Yet at the end, there's that final line: "I am free," a type of affirmation that reinforces the goal. These lines also contain parallel structure with the repetition of "as"—phrases that explain the actions of the spell.

Here are some other ways to create rhythm using repetition:

- *Connectives* employ the use of words like *and* over and over for effect. This example also uses parallelism: a convention that reinforces an image by building upon it over and over again.

The sun rises and touches the world; the light hallows and heals us; its warmth feeds and sustains us.

- *Parataxis* is "setting side by side" without conjunctions.

Water, wash over me, rain down on me, cover me, cleanse me, make me new.

- *Anaphora* is the repetition of the same word or phrase at the beginning of lines or sentences. *Repetend* uses the repetition of a word or phrase at various places throughout the piece (middle or end).

Brigit, hear me,

Brigit, console me,

Brigit, empower me.

Fire of life, give me the spark I need.

Fire of life, give me the power I need.

Here's an example that utilizes several features of repetition without end rhymes. In this piece, the phrase "to make magic is" is repeated at the beginning of some lines but not all of them. The word "to" is also used frequently. These things create rhythm. Also note the use of internal rhyme—for example, "receive" and "believe," "explore" and "core," and "places" and "faces."

To make magic is

to offer and to receive,

to question and wonder but also

believe that anything is possible.

To make magic is

to become whole, to explore,

to split yourself to the core of your being;

to discover deep, dark places and pull the masks

off the faces of the gods;

to realize you are one with the universe

and all it contains, know there's a web

at the root of all things that cannot be broken.

To make magic is

to honor, love, and speak your truth;

to seek and never stop looking, to understand

yourself as much as you can at this moment.

To make magic is to change the world.

Word order and arrangement is called *syntax,* and this choice can make your writing more precise and powerful. Here are some arrangements to consider:

- *Parallel statements* are balanced statements that can give your spoken chants and spells a very pleasing rhythm without even using rhyme. There's an ebb and flow to the words, and it is accomplished by repeating words and groups of words (see *chiasmus*). "I seek solace in the light, and in the light I shine."
- The *chiasmus* technique is a repetition of a pattern or word(s) in reverse order—the most popular example is "When the going gets tough, the tough get going."
- *Asyndeton* is to omit conjunctions (for, and, nor, but, or, yet, so), as in "I came, I saw, I conquered."[108]
- *Epistrophe* is the repetition of words or phrases at the ends of sentences. An example of this is "Government of the people, by the people, and for the people."[109]
- Lastly, consider *triplets*. We all know the importance of trinities. If balance is a rhythm of two, then threes create rhythm by using the feature of listing. In ancient curses, for example, a word's power "could be increased by a variety of rhetorical devices, such as repetition, rhythm, and the use of triplets."[110] Use these in your words, both spoken and written (see chapter 17). The series of words should do more than merely list things; it should build upon connected ideas or images. The Serenity Prayer is also a good example: "Grant me the serenity to accept the things I cannot change, the courage to change the things I can, and the wisdom to know the difference." The following seed blessing incorporates the growing cycle by using a triplet pattern:

Let these seeds be nurtured to set root,

encouraged by the sun to reach the sky,

and bear the fruit to start new life again.

108. Julius Caesar, "Veni, Vidi, Vici," Oxford Learner's Dictionaries, accessed May 24, 2024, https://www.oxfordlearnersdictionaries.com/us/definition/english/veni-vidi-vici.

109. Abraham Lincoln, "Gettysburg Address," Library of Congress, accessed May 24, 2024, https://www.loc.gov/resource/rbpe.24404500/?st=text.

110. J. H. M. Strubbe, "Cursed Be He That Moves My Bones," in *Magika Hiera: Ancient Greek Magic and Religion*, ed. Christopher A. Faraone and Dirk Obbink (New York: Oxford University Press, 1991), 41.

Not every piece you write needs to have perfect rhythm. But when you know you're going to be chanting the words, it's worth giving this aspect some consideration. Even if you're not planning to chant the words repeatedly, speaking your spell out loud is part of the magic, and the rhythm can affect the overall impact of the piece as you recite it. In chapter 7, we will give some attention to the actual act of speaking and performance of your words.

Word-Witch Practice
Rhythm

For your rhythm practice, try a few of these exercises.

- Take one of your existing chants and read it aloud, checking for any places where you can improve the rhythm. Count the syllables in each line and/or divide up the lines in new ways.

- Create some phrases that experiment with parallel statements, chiasmus, triplets, etc. Use the lists of words you created in chapter 5 to come up with ideas.

- Create a chant that repeats the same word or phrase over and over to raise energy.

- Go outside and listen. What natural rhythms and patterns can you detect in nature: the buzzing of insects, the chirping of frogs, birdsongs, wind, rain, etc.? Try this during different times of the day and in different seasons. In addition, don't overlook visual patterns too. Nature is filled with rhythmic pattern.

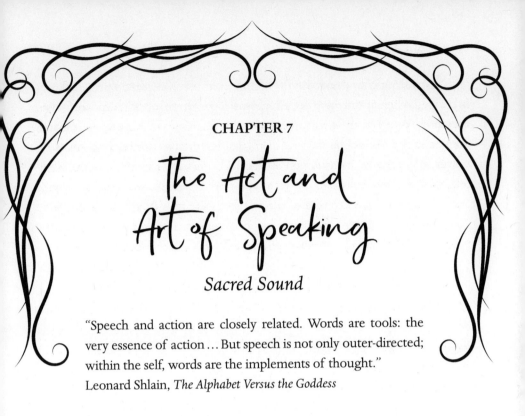

CHAPTER 7

The Act and Art of Speaking

Sacred Sound

"Speech and action are closely related. Words are tools: the very essence of action ... But speech is not only outer-directed; within the self, words are the implements of thought."
Leonard Shlain, *The Alphabet Versus the Goddess*

Using words in magic effectively involves more than using the most appropriate combination of words and sounds. *How* you say the words is important as well.

In the study of mythology, there is a term called *ex nihilo*, which means "out of nothing," and it refers to the type of creation myth where the world is created by a deity making the world from nothing. This act can involve many things but often includes speaking—the act of words creating order from chaos. Think of your speech during ritual and spellwork as the work of creation—it's sacred; it's formed with the breath of life. Breathe that life into your words. Visualize your voice carrying magic—it *is* magic. It's part of your essence. This goes for all sounds—humming, whistling, etc. If it helps, visualize each word and sound carrying your will and intent; the air that creates each word is the breath of life itself, and it is sacred.

Consider people who are voice talents—people who can change their voice, such as actors, or those who can imitate others, create animal sounds, replicate accents and dialects. This takes practice. Have you ever experimented with your voice this way? Have you ever pretended to have an accent or raised or lowered your voice to imitate someone? Or maybe you've experimented with portraying characters while reading out loud? You can do similar things in magic. When performing a spell, prayer, incantation, or other spoken verse, decide if you need to whisper or shout, for example, or have your voice be commanding or humble. If "trying on" a different voice makes you feel more powerful, do it. Also, consider speed—record yourself and see how you sound. Adjust your pace depending on what you're reciting. Practice making sounds and saying words. Notice where your tongue is and how your lips are shaped.

This chapter covers a variety of techniques concerning how you use your voice and ways to pay attention to the sounds you make when speaking.

Direction and Emphasis

Most of us don't hear ourselves speak out loud on a regular basis, and when we do, we don't like the way we sound, or we're surprised that our voice sounds so different from the way we thought it would. I've gotten used to this over the years, especially when I started teaching online classes and making video lectures. I can say from experience that it's worth it to record yourself and listen—it will help you train your voice and improve your speech. And this will strengthen your magical voice.

Whatever your style, when you speak with magical intent, confidence is key, even if you're only mouthing the words or whispering. Pay attention to your breath; notice all the parts of your body that are engaged when you speak or sing. Feel where the sound comes from—diaphragm, chest, throat. Embody the words, become them—do more than recite them. You are creating them, making them with your body. Giving full attention to the act of speaking can enhance all aspects of your magical experience. Don't forget about your posture. Sit or stand up straight to allow for strong air flow. If you have experience with music, either singing or playing a wind instrument, you probably already have a good understanding of these practices.

Now let's take a closer look at where your words are going. To whom are you speaking? It may seem like an obvious question, but it deserves attention. Are you addressing the universe, a deity, your higher self? Are you charging an object such as an amulet? It makes a difference in your approach. Let's use the analogy of your "target audience" and consider how to "direct" your speech.

To send out your goal to the universe, you could speak into the wind and visualize your words going out into the world. If you're speaking to a deity, you can use an image, statue, or your imagination. For an object, speak over it or into it (this includes stones, shells, food and drink, candles, etc.). For self-affirmations, you could address yourself in the mirror. You can project or direct your voice to a specific place, for example: toward the sky, at an object, or into the wind or water. You can cup your hands around your mouth and shout; you can whistle or hum. Additionally, considering direction will also help you decide on tone of voice and style of speaking.

Illnesses were once viewed as having a "personality" that could "respond to a command."[111] Charms and spells could be addressed toward the disease they were intended to cure; plants, celestial bodies, spirits, and even inanimate objects could be addressed with words. The point is that the words are addressed to something or someone. When you speak, consider where your voice is going—where, to whom or what. Also consider how you should address that being or object, what you are bringing into existence, or what you are creating or commanding.

While we're on the subject of where to direct your speech, we should also consider where you're drawing your energy or magical power from. This can not only aid visualization; it can also guide your words with more precision. I like to think of everything as a web of energy, of which we are but a small part. The Divine or Universal Consciousness is that web, and there are strands that connect everything. Your personal power and energy are the source of your magic, but they're also part of the larger network that links everything together, so you can draw on that energy too. If it helps, you can visualize a specific Element that pertains to your spell or a deity. Think of it like an energy exchange—a flow that travels in many directions, not just one way. Each person or thing—tree, stone, etc.—has its particular energy, but again, we're all linked. We're all collections of vibrating particles. Since everything is connected, you can imagine your energy and the Universal Consciousness intertwining. You can visualize specific parts of the body that are engaged in the recitation (see chapter 10, Words and Chakras section). You can even use your words to "narrate" the process. You can say things like the following:

---

111. Kieckhefer, *Magic in the Middle Ages*.

Let my words transmit my will into this [stone or other item]…

My words connect me to the [Universe or Divine] and, thus,
   to all things in the world.

My voice carries my intent…

My words manifest my goal…

With these words I speak, let my purpose be fulfilled…

My words and actions ripple through the web of life
   and have the power to make change…

Plotinus explains in his *Enneads* that prayer and magic both operate via "natural sympathetic bonds within the universe," thus creating a "living network of influences."[112] In animistic cultures, all things are believed to have a spirit—rocks, trees, lakes, etc. This is one explanation for magic: that it comes from the power all around us and particular plants and stones contain a personality or properties useful for specific actions or qualities. Others would say it originates in deity, the cosmos, the universe, or celestial bodies.[113] And still others say it comes from within us. It could be all of these. The important question is, What do *you* think?

Sound Frequency

How often do you consider the mechanics of human speech? We take it for granted until something happens and we lose our voice. It seems like such a simple thing: we talk, whisper, shout, laugh, whistle, sing—processes that involve many biological functions. Our bodies are like musical instruments made of muscle, flesh, and bone, and words can be thought to have a "mind (their meanings) but also a body—the structure of sound in which their meaning lives."[114] To fully experience words, we need to, as *The Poet's Companion* puts it, "let the language vibrate through our rib cage and vocal chords…savor the delicious taste of syllables on our tongue."[115]

---

112. Kieckhefer, *Magic in the Middle Ages.*

113. Kieckhefer, *Magic in the Middle Ages.*

114. John Frederick Nims and David Mason, *Western Wind: An Introduction to Poetry*, 4th ed. (Boston, MA: McGraw-Hill, 2000), 151.

115. Addonizio and Laux, *The Poet's Companion*, 139–40.

We call the sounds that create speech *phonemes*. They are the smallest unit of sound that we use to make all our words. We use shapes—letters—in order to write sounds, and those are called *graphemes*. Most linguists have agreed upon forty-four basic sounds in the English language, with a few differences here and there based on accents. And the English alphabet contains twenty-six letters used to represent those forty-four sounds and all their spelling variations.

Let's take a moment to consider the fascinating mechanics of human speech. The study of voice acoustics reveals that there are myriad ways to make sound, but we probably don't think much about this on a daily basis. It's actually a very complex process, not to mention the act of hearing the sounds as well (but that's another issue).

In simplest terms, sound begins with air from our lungs. This air passes through the vocal cords (the actual term is *vocal folds*), causing them to vibrate. If you touch your throat while humming, you can feel it. You can also feel the change in vibration if you hum, speak, or sing in a higher or lower tone (frequency). When you whisper, there is no vibration—try it. It's really interesting to experiment with sound this way. We can make sounds that are "voiced" and sounds that are "unvoiced."

When we actually produce voiced sound, there are several parts of the body involved—our tongue, lips, and nasal cavity, plus other things you may not be aware of. Try making sounds like a sustained "s," "sh," or "z," for example, or saying letters like "t," "b," "f," and "g." Notice how your mouth changes shape. Say the word *trip* and pay attention to the position of your tongue and lips. Play with other words and sounds. Your mouth acts as a filter, controlling how much sound gets through and also changing the frequency of that sound. In addition to the basic consonants and vowels, there are also "liquid" sounds ("r" and "l") and "nasal" sounds ("n," "m," "ng," "gn"). Try making these sounds. We vary our pitch when we make sounds by changing the muscle tension and pressure.[116]

Scientifically, we know that we hear sounds because of sound waves reaching our ears. But here's something interesting: studies have shown that reading silently produces similar effects to saying words out loud. Scientists have

---

116. Joe Wolfe, Maëva Garnier, and John Smith, "Voice Acoustics: An Introduction," Music Acoustics, University of New South Wales, accessed April 8, 2024, http://newt.phys.unsw.edu.au/jw/voice.html.

identified that "tiny wires attached to the speech areas of the throat have picked up electrical currents—evidence that the muscles were being stimulated during silent reading. The body participates sympathetically with what it experiences."[117] We know that color has been proven to affect mood—sound affects us as well. Babies even react to sound in the womb.

Vowels can be compared to musical chords, making up "tones and overtones from the resonating system of throat, mouth, and head."[118] Sound waves differ in length, giving us what we perceive as higher and lower sounds (short waves are high; long waves are slow). One thing that's really interesting about this is that many words "sound" like what they are—for example, *light* and *bright* or *gloom* and *doom*—the "i" sound is lighter, and the "oo" is darker. The lighter sounds (high frequency) actually sound and feel higher, and the darker ones (low frequency) sound and feel lower.

High-frequency sounds lift us up and encourage us; they are exciting. Low notes are also related to larger objects but can also be felt as powerful or ominous.[119] Think of caves. Have you ever spoken in a cavern or large empty room and felt the enormity of the space around you? The way we make sound doesn't only concern our mouth but also our head. It's like a resonating chamber. Make the sound "ee," then make the sound "oh" or "ah." The higher sound of "ee" doesn't resonate as much—it's a "smaller" sound. The "ah" is a larger one and actually takes up more space in the mouth.[120] You can think of each vowel sound as having a characteristic like this—a personality. When you make a vowel sound, the breath flows. Say, "a, e, i, o, u." You can move from one to the other without a "stop"—the way you stop air flow when making consonant sounds. Additionally, think of sounds in nature. The sounds of an avalanche or stormy waters reverberate lower than the sounds of rain or hail on a rooftop.[121]

117. Nims and Mason, *Western Wind*, 152.

118. Nims and Mason, *Western Wind*, 154.

119. Nims and Mason, *Western Wind*, 157.

120. Nims and Mason, *Western Wind*, 157–58.

121. Nims and Mason, *Western Wind*, 157.

Word-Witch Practice
The Act and Art of Speaking

To practice the techniques discussed in this chapter, here are some activities to try.

- Record yourself. Begin by talking (say whatever you'd like), then move on to reading a passage of text (anything—fiction, the news), and, finally, recite a chant or other piece you've written. Experiment and see what it sounds like when you raise or lower your voice, try an accent, etc. Read a short story and pretend to be the characters. Perform a few pages of your favorite book as though you're recording an audio version. Really listen to yourself when you play it back and be honest about what you hear. How do you sound? Can you project confidence? Emotion? Energy?

- Experiment with making a variety of sounds and noticing where they come from in your body. Put your hand on your stomach, chest, throat. Observe where the sounds come from when you sing, shout, whisper, etc.

- Imagine the web of Consciousness/Universe and your connection to it. Meditate on this. Visualize your words being connected to it in whatever way makes the most sense to you. Remember: you can create magic with your words—the air, the breath, is sacred.

- Practice visualizing your words. One way to do this is imagine the words coming out of your mouth as letters. Really try to see them and the words they create. Visualize the direction you intend them to go; see them floating there, whether it's somewhere inside you or near you, or somewhere far away. Visualize the words as actual arrangements of letters floating through the air.

- It's worth noting that the "ah" sound is the most basic, primal sound humans make—it's universal.[122] Consider this aspect as you work with the magic of sound.

---

122. John McWhorter, *Ancient Writing and the History of the Alphabet* (Chantilly: The Teaching Company, 2023), 32.

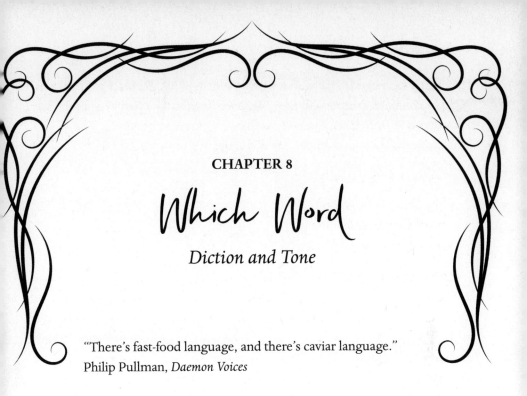

CHAPTER 8

Which Word

Diction and Tone

"There's fast-food language, and there's caviar language."
Philip Pullman, *Daemon Voices*

Tone is defined as the attitude of the author toward the subject. We often use a reverent tone in rituals and prayers, but many of us feel a very personal connection in our spiritual practice and are comfortable using a conversational tone—just "talking" to deity, the universe, etc. Use whatever you feel is the most appropriate for the situation. You might use casual speech for an impromptu prayer and formal language in a ritual. In spoken magic, consider the tone of your voice. As we discussed in the previous chapter, do you need to be soft or loud, whisper or shout, be commanding or humble? Are your words a formal address or casual speech? Practice using your voice effectively; record yourself and experiment. A whisper can still be powerful; a shout can lack conviction. Always put your emotions and intent behind your words.

Word Choice

Word choice is called *diction*, and as a writing teacher, one of the most significant concepts I try to convey to students is how important it is to choose the most appropriate word. This takes practice. Expanding your vocabulary doesn't happen overnight—it comes from reading and writing, in addition to looking up new words and, yes, using a thesaurus.[123] Word choice is important because diction also expresses tone. We all know how the same word or phrase spoken in a different tone can take on an entirely new meaning.

Let's return to the example I used in chapter 6:

Inspiration come to me,

keep me reaching higher.

Give me everything I need,

grant me my desire.

This spell is asking for something from the universe. The phrase "come to me" is confident but not commanding. The "keep me reaching higher" line is asking for the strength to keep striving to reach the goal. "Give me everything I need," again, is asking, but the word "give" may be somewhat demanding. Perhaps a better word would be "bring" or maybe "show." "Grant me my desire" is a gentle plea for something. Making demands is not the same thing as being confident. Be assertive, but not pushy—just as in real life. Be sincere and project a respectful attitude toward the universe or the deity you are addressing.

Here's another example using two versions of a short affirmation:

I am inspired. I keep reaching higher to achieve my desire.

I am inspired. I will reach higher and achieve my desire.

The words in these affirmations are even more positive than the previous example, stating rather than asking for inspiration to "come." There's no doubt here—the desire will be achieved. While both pieces use the present tense, the affirmations are more active. Instead of "reaching higher to achieve," the words state "I *am* inspired." And the second affirmation is even more specific: more than "I keep reaching higher," the statement is "I *will* reach higher *and* achieve." It may not seem like a dramatic difference, but even just one word can shift your awareness.

---

123. When using a thesaurus to find new words, be sure you understand the subtleties of each word's meaning and any connotations it may have. Don't just choose words at random—be sure you understand what they mean.

Affirmations are a little like being your own cheerleader—a way of giving yourself a pep talk. Or think of them like saying it makes it true. It has happened already. Saying these words aloud, confidently, is important. Don't whisper them with your head down. Visualize your goal and know that it is going to happen. In this case, the "desire" would be something very specific. Perhaps you're an artist or writer seeking publication—visualize your first piece in an art show or your book being published. If you need help finding the most precise word for your goal, use a thesaurus. There are several online ones that are quite good—some even have a rhyming feature as well. An affirmation states that it will happen. For example, instead of asking, "Help me get the job," say, "I will get the job." Then state, specifically, what the job is and where.

For another example of the subtle differences in word choice, consider these words: *clothed, dressed, wrapped, cloaked*. They all sort of mean the same thing, but each has its own personality or connotation. The words *clothed* and *dressed* imply the wearing of clothing; *wrapped* could be anything—fabric, paper on a package; *cloaked* implies secrecy.

I once wrote a poem that contained these lines:

endings and beginnings
are of the same substance
clothed in different disguises

Later, I changed "clothed" to "dressed" for the sake of alliteration: "dressed in different disguises," and then I wondered if the word "guises" would be more appropriate than "disguises." So I consulted a dictionary for the precise definitions: *guise*, noun, "the appearance of someone or something, especially when intended to deceive"; *disguise*, noun, "to give a new appearance to a person or thing, especially in order to hide its true form."[124] Both words involve hiding something. Both words would be appropriate in this situation. I thought I preferred "dressed in different guises," but then I changed it back to "disguises" after returning to the piece later. If this all seems a bit tedious, it's part of the

---

124. "Guise," Cambridge English Dictionary, Cambridge University Press & Assessment, accessed July 16, 2024, https://dictionary.cambridge.org/us/dictionary/english/guise; "Disguise," Cambridge English Dictionary, Cambridge University Press & Assessment, accessed July 16, 2024, https://dictionary.cambridge.org/us/dictionary/english/disguise.

revision process to "re-see" something and reconsider our words. The key is to find a balance between revising and not obsessing over every single word. But tinkering with a piece to get it just right can be rewarding.

Always consider the denotations and connotations of your words. *Denotation* is the literal, dictionary meaning of a word. *Connotation* means the "baggage" associated with words. Here's an example: When we hear the word *discriminate*, most of us automatically think of prejudice. That is one of its meanings, and it has a negative connotation. The other definition of discriminate means "to recognize distinctions," such as being a discriminating shopper, choosing one thing over another based on noticing differences. Being aware of these distinctions can help you choose the most precise words for your goal.

Another important aspect of word choice involves knowing when to be specific and when to be general. For example, if you're hoping to find a job but don't have a specific one in mind, your approach should be general, keeping all possibilities open. But if you've found something specific you want, visualize that and say it.

The use of abstract or concrete words also deserves some attention. Abstract words are things like love, freedom, happiness—concepts. Concrete words are usually tangible things—things you see or touch, like an object. Choosing the most appropriate words for your spells helps direct your energy and gives it precision.

Sometimes you want to be general in order to include a wide array of options and scenarios. Often, we want to leave things open to the universe. For example, consider this general morning or evening prayer:

Spirits divine
of moon and sun,
bless me and mine
[now day has begun or now day is done].

This prayer asks for a general blessing, which could include a variety of things. In this case, we want to leave it open for interpretation. However, you could modify this to ask for protection instead of asking for a general blessing. Instead of "spirits," you could also say, "Lord and Lady," use names of deities, or simply address the universe.

But sometimes we want to be very specific. If you're creating a spell for protection, you must ask yourself, What are you seeking to protect? Your home? A vehicle? Is it yourself in a specific situation? An object? This will determine not only your style but will make a difference in your word choice. You might want to incorporate words like *protect, shield, guard, safe,* or *keep.*

For example, when saying, "Protect this home and all within," the words "all within" include both people and objects, but you can take it a step further if you want and say, "all people, pets, and objects." Instead of "I will succeed," you may want to define what that success means. Be specific. Does success mean getting the job or just getting the interview? Of course, sometimes it's okay to be general when looking for love or spells for good fortune.

Here's a spell I wrote many years ago for protection while traveling. These are just the recited words; the entire spell requires additional action (it's a crystal and candle spell).

Great Spirit, bless my family, protect us while apart.

No matter where we are, home is in our hearts.

Great Spirit, guide my travels by land or sky or sea.

Safe journey, safe return—so mote it be.

The last line is intended to be a refrain, repeated several times.

Note that this is a spell for travel that includes land, sky, and sea. It asks for blessings and protection for the traveler but also considers the family at home. It also mentions the journey and the return.

And finally, consider levels of formality. As mentioned in the section on tone, think of "dressing" your language the way you put on clothes for various occasions. Do you need to be formal or casual? Precise or spontaneous? Confident or humble?[125]

Of course, your personal style will also direct you; some people prefer general words and use their visualization for specifics. But I always like to make my intent as clear as possible to the universe just in case, so there's no doubt, no question.

Consider these two phrases:

---

125. For a deeper look at linguistics and magic, I recommend Patrick Dunn's book *Magic, Power, Language, Symbol.*

Dispel my fear.

Give me courage.

Both of these imply the same thing, but with a different approach. Getting rid of fear is a type of banishing, overcoming it, or sending it away. Increasing courage is drawing something to you. But the word "fear" itself contains negativity. The choice is ultimately yours. You could use numerology to decide (see chapter 17). You could tackle it from both angles and do spells for both. The second line rewrites the phrase, so the word "fear" isn't even included. You could also say: "I have courage," "I am strong," or even "I've got this!"

Taboo Words

Cultures deem some words so powerful that we dare not utter them. Most of these are words of a derogatory or insulting nature; we know that, depending on one's culture, certain words are offensive. Again, words have the power to hurt. But let's consider some taboo words that are useful in certain situations. Think of how you felt the first time you used a curse word. Did you feel empowered? Like you were breaking the rules? What is considered vulgar language has changed throughout history, and what's considered acceptable depends on the situation.

One research study has concluded that swear words make up 0.3–0.5 percent of the words people use every day—that's one word for every two hundred to three hundred.[126] Profanity is as old as language itself, and there may be a good reason for its use. Our bodies react physically when we hear these types of words, depending on the individual situation. Curse words can actually help us process emotions.

> A fascinating study, published in 2009 in the journal *NeuroReport* by researchers at Keele University, demonstrated that swearing may not only express pain but help relieve it. Many linguists have tried to explain this phenomenon, and part of the reason may be that expletives are stored in a different part of the brain (the right hemisphere) than the rest of language (in left hemisphere). Swear words may acti-

---

126. Anne Curzan, *The Secret Life of Words: English Words and Their Origins* (Chantilly, VA: The Teaching Company, 2012), 231.

vate the amygdala, triggering the fight-or-flight response, which dulls pain.[127]

Our use of these words doesn't always make sense; it eludes logic but has an impact on us. In a PET scan, the speaking of ordinary words lights up parts of the left brain, the area related to logic. But when speaking curse words, parts of the right brain light up, areas associated with expressing emotion. Curse words are impulsive, often popping out of us when surprised or startled, or during moments of frustration, anger, or even delight. According to linguist John McWhorter in his book titled *Nine Nasty Words*, "profanity channels our essence."[128]

The significance of using this language can be seen by our use of "swearing" as a synonym for profanity—a holdover from the past when a "swear" held more weight. In medieval times, a "swear" was an actual oath or promise to God—like a signature in an oral society—and meant to be sincere. One remnant we still have today is the act of "being sworn in" for a legal proceeding. Many odd phrases and expressions have come from attempts to veil swearing, such as "jeepers creepers," "gee," or "geez" was used to avoid exclaiming "Jesus Christ!"[129] "Oh my gosh" was used instead of "oh my god"—although today these are not typically considered obscene. And the word *damn* is from *damnare* (Latin), "to condemn"; it evolved, as words do. While there are lots of folk etymologies floating around about the origins of curse words, the actual history of their origins and usage is unremarkable, but still interesting.

Words have the power we give them, and while the styles and usage may change over time and vary between cultures, the fact that we have taboo words is fundamental to our social consciousness—they are cathartic expressions.[130] But some words—those used for the slander of certain groups—are much more serious and harmful than others. According to McWhorter, there

---

127. Curzan, *The Secret Life of Words*, 231–32; Richard Stephens, John Atkins, and Andrew Kingston, "Swearing as a Response to Pain," *NeuroReport* 20, no. 12 (August 5, 2009): 1056–1060, www.doi.org/10.1097/WNR.0b013e32832e64b1; Timothy Jay, "The Utility and Ubiquity of Taboo Words," *Perspectives on Psychological Science* 4, no. 2 (March 2009): 153, https://doi.org/10.1111/j.1745-6924.2009.01115.x.

128. John McWhorter, *Nine Nasty Words: English in the Gutter: Then, Now, and Forever* (New York: Random House, 2021), 4, 2.

129. McWhorter, *Nine Nasty Words*, 23.

130. McWhorter, *Nine Nasty Words*, 4.

has been a progression throughout history of three types of profanity, when the worst things you could say were (1) on the topic of religion, (2) things about the body, and (3) insults to groups of people.[131] For these reasons, using taboo words in magic is very subjective.

So how can you, or should you, use taboo words in magic? It depends. It can be cathartic to utter an expression that feels inappropriate, like dropping an f-bomb in church. Our use of language makes us human and can help us express the wide spectrum of feelings we have, sometimes even mixed emotions we otherwise don't know how to convey. Yet some may consider it disrespectful. This is, as with all aspects of your magical practice, your call. And it will depend on each specific situation. All I can say is try it and see if it appeals to you.

For some people, these words are part of everyday usage already; for others, using them is a real expression of strong emotion. And, of course, we can use them for comedic effect. While we should take words seriously, we should also be able to laugh at ourselves and understand that breaking taboos and crossing boundaries is part of what makes us human, and can even help our emotional growth.

Word-Witch Practice
Diction

Use these activities to explore the concept of diction in your magical writing.

- Using the lists of words you created in chapter 5, use a thesaurus to find similar words you could use instead, and write down the differences between the words. For example, *storm*, *wind*, *breeze*, and *tempest* are similar but have subtle differences. Which one is most appropriate for your piece?

- Examine previous pieces you've written and experiment with using different words.

- Consider how you feel about using taboo words in your magical practice; experiment with it.

---

131. McWhorter, *Nine Nasty Words*, 8–9.

- Make lists of homonyms—see how many you can come up with. (See One-Word Spell in chapter 11.)
- Make lists of abstractions that you can represent with specific, concrete items, activities, or more specific language. For example, *freedom—flag, protest, breaking bonds* or *impermanence—turn to dust, fade away, dissolve.*
- Make lists of generalities that you can clarify with specific things. For example, *fruit—bananas, peaches* or *flowers—roses, violets, tulips.*
- Make a list of uncertain words and statements that you can flip to something positive: *I hope I can ...* or *I know I can ...* Or make a list of opposites: *fear* vs. *courage* or *despair* vs. *hope.*

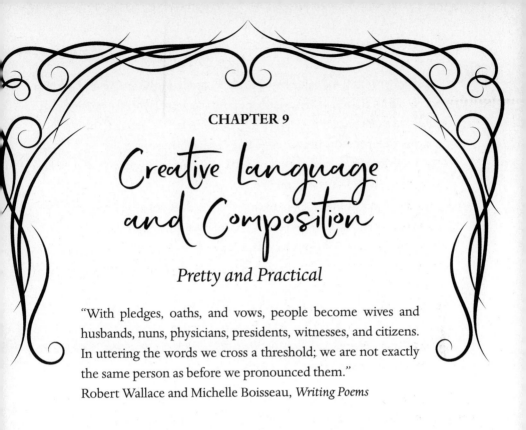

CHAPTER 9

Creative Language and Composition

Pretty and Practical

"With pledges, oaths, and vows, people become wives and husbands, nuns, physicians, presidents, witnesses, and citizens. In uttering the words we cross a threshold; we are not exactly the same person as before we pronounced them."
Robert Wallace and Michelle Boisseau, *Writing Poems*

The basics of rhyme and rhythm can help you create a solid verse for chanting, and word choice gives you precision, but what if you want to do even more? The next step is to make your language sparkle. Figurative language involves all sorts of techniques that writers use to create interesting images and evoke emotions. You don't have to use it, but it can add an extra layer of creativity to your work.

Figurative Language

These are probably techniques you are familiar with, but let's take a closer look:

- *Personification* is attributing human qualities to nonhuman things. This is probably the technique I use the most when writing for magical purposes. This is a perfect way to describe the spiritual connection we have with nature.

- *Metaphor* and *simile* are comparisons—both techniques compare something to something else, but simile uses *like* or *as*, and a metaphor doesn't. *Analogy* is another way to compare things, but in this case, the purpose is often to compare something familiar to something unfamiliar in order to clarify an explanation. For example, *climbing the corporate ladder* uses the concept of a ladder to represent advancement. Comparing river systems to the branches of trees is also an analogy. The act of sympathetic magic itself is a kind of analogy—taking action that represents the desired outcome of the spell.

- *Symbols* are simply concrete objects that stand for abstract concepts, such as a heart shape representing love. In crafting your magical work, you can add layers of meaning by using an object to represent something else. There are many popular symbols you already know, such as the moon representing the cycles of life, particular animals that stand for certain characteristics (the lion symbolizes strength), or fire representing the "spark" of creativity or desire. In fact, utilizing the four Elements is a good way to begin using symbolism since each of them has associations with abstract ideas (see chapter 20).

Using figurative language is a wonderful way to create rich descriptions for prayers, invocations, and other pieces. There's nothing wrong with using easy phrases like *swift as the wind*, but it's fun to create new and interesting ways of saying things—make your descriptions unique and suitable to your style. In one of my pieces titled "Worm Moon" (see chapter 19), simile is used to describe the moon as being "cradled like a pearl." This phrase from another one of my poems is a metaphor: "The body of a god / is the title of an old song without words."

Sympathetic magic is all about something representing something else. This is the perfect opportunity to use comparison or symbolism. Here are some examples of experimenting with creative language to evoke vivid images. Let's say you're creating a protection spell using candles and thorns. In the written portion or the chant, you can refer to the components of the spell by listing them and the role they serve, or narrate the process of lighting candles, etc., but you can make this part even more creative by using comparison and other techniques.

Instead of simply saying:

By this fire and these thorns, I am kept safe from harm.

You could use a metaphor to say:

These candles are a wall of fire surrounding and protecting me ... these thorns are an impenetrable, tangled briar ...

You can also use simile and create a rhyming chant with a refrain:

These thorns, like a tangled briar,
repel all harm.
These candles, like a wall of fire,
repel all harm.

The phrases could also be made shorter, and the word "like" could be omitted:

Thorny branches, tangled briar;
row of candles, wall of fire.

You could write down the name or names of what you are asking for protection from, place the candles on the paper, surround everything with thorny branches (from roses, for example), then say:

Strength of thorn and heat of flame,
protect me from the [thing or one(s)] I've named.

Another method would be to write a detailed explanation of the spell goal on the paper, explaining who needs protection from what or whom, and then use a chant as reinforcement. Even better—write on handmade paper with a magically charged pen, ink, or a pencil (see chapters 12 and 13).

The point is to consider doing more than mentioning the items you're using and their purpose.

Many spells use the words "by the power of." For example, "By the power of this flowing stream, I am purified and clean." But you can also say, "Like the water of this stream, I am purified and clean," comparing yourself to the item. Here are some other examples:

Like this stone, I'm standing strong.
Like the great oak, I'm grounded yet reaching for the sky.

Also common are narrating the actions of the spell, asking for the item (crystal, herb, etc.) to bring you something or have some effect, or statements and affirmations that declare the action is happening. And while it's fine to say, "Lavender, calm and soothe me ..." you could say, "Lavender, with your gentle sway, kindly send my cares away" (if you like to rhyme). Instead of phrases like "Dispel my worries," you could say, "Relaxation washes over me like a wave." Consider including words that describe the qualities of the aroma: "calm and sweet," "uplifting," "peaceful," etc. When describing an action, see if you can make it more descriptive and creative. Be as specific as you can.

We often say things like "As this candle melts, so do my fears ..." or "This candle represents [the fear], and as it burns [the intent]." And again, there's nothing wrong with that. But with some figurative language (and rhyme), we get a more creative and specific statement:

Melting wax, melting fears,
as this candle disappears
my fears dissolve, destroyed by flame—
now I list them all by name:
[state fears to be conquered].

Instead of a general statement about the action of seed planting to represent success and growth:

The planting of this seed is the planting of my goal, as it grows, so does ...

You could use comparison:

My success grows like the oak from the acorn ...
My potential is the acorn growing into the greatest oak ...

Or:

Dandelion seeds, feathered dreams, wishes on wings ...
As these seeds take flight on the wind, each one is a wish I send ...

Here's an example that uses personification. This piece doesn't use a particular rhyming pattern, but note the musical effect created by the sound of the words. This is a poem that can also serve as a spell—that's the intent I had when I wrote it. I wanted to write a spell that was a little more complex than what I typically write; I wanted it to be more poetic but still have the qualities of a spell. And yet someone could read it as a poem, and it still works.

Spell for a Stormy Day
As the wind shakes the branches
let it, too, stir something new
and good in my life;
> *may it bring only things I want or need*
> *and let it take away*
whatever's holding me back.
May it touch me
the way it touches water—
> *telling it sweet secrets,*
> *making it laugh in ripples.*
May the rain renew me
in ways I never knew I needed,
streaming down until the spent sky opens—
> *and when the thunder speaks*
> *I will understand*
the language of the storm.

Note that some of the lines are indented a few spaces. This technique is used to either heighten a pause or to draw attention to a word or phrase, setting it apart from the others. Think of it almost like starting a new paragraph, but without breaking the stanza. Some of the word choice is general because the spell is asking for the removal of anything and everything that is "holding me back," leaving it open for things the speaker may or may not be aware of. And yet there is a specific intent: renewal, the seeking of something new.

These techniques are especially well suited to magic. The images we create with words, the suggestions and comparisons, are just one more way to spark the creativity of magic and aid visualization. Using words this way can help us imagine more than what we see and consider our world in new ways. With figurative language, you are literally creating something new, something unique to your perspective. This, too, can be an act of discovery, an invitation to wonder.

Punctuation

I notice grammar—it comes with the territory of being an English professor. But sometimes rules are more like guidelines, and sometimes guidelines can be bent in the name of style. But there's one area that governs nearly everything I write, and that is punctuation (again, as more of a guideline than a rule). Even when I write short phrases for chanting, I put in commas, periods, dashes, and semicolons. It's not because I'm a stickler for a perfect sentence; it's because punctuation guides the reading and recitation process. Like rests, time signatures, and breath marks serve as a guide when reading music, punctuation marks are cues that tell us where to pause, breathe, stop, etc. These marks can control the rhythm of a piece and help others read it as well. In fact, "for a millennium and a half, punctuation's purpose was to guide actors, chanters and readers-aloud through stretches of manuscript, indicating the pauses, accentuating matters of sense and sound."[132] As the title of the popular book on grammar, *Eats, Shoots & Leaves*, reminds us—the placement of a comma can entirely change the meaning of a sentence. Here's one of the examples from the book: "The convict said the judge is mad." It's entirely different to say, "The convict, said the judge, is mad."[133]

Here's another subtle example of just changing the punctuation, again from Truss's book.[134]

"'Verily, I say unto thee, This day thou shalt be with me in Paradise.'"

"'Verily I say unto thee this day, Thou shalt be with me in Paradise.'"

Look at the commas. See the difference punctuation can make?

This is why I encourage you to consider punctuation—especially if you're writing a long piece or plan to lead a group recitation. A few short lines that are complete thoughts probably don't need punctuation as much as others. In

---

132. Lynne Truss, *Eats, Shoots & Leaves* (New York: Gotham Books, 2003), 72.

133. Cecil Hartley, *Principles of Punctuation: or, The Art of Pointing* (Effingham Wilson, 1818), quoted in Truss, *Eats, Shoots & Leaves*, 97.

134. Truss, *Eats, Shoots & Leaves*, 74.

many cases, a line break can serve as a pause. Lack of punctuation can some-times even impede the meaning of a phrase, so it often helps to have it.

Pauses can also help create rhythm. In addition to the period that ends a sentence, punctuation within a sentence, such as a comma or dash, can be use-ful as well. These can help give time for silence and "as musicians know, silence is an integral part of the music."[135] A pause, a moment of silence, can be power-ful. But, since everyone reads differently, performance will always be an individ-ual act.

There's one more term I'd like to include here and that's *caesura*. This term is used in poetry (and also in music) to refer to a pause, rest, or place to take a breath. It can occur between phrases and is often marked by punctuation, but not always. In long sentences, it's worth experimenting with recitation to find the best place for a pause. Understanding the art of a well-placed pause can add to the rhythmic quality of your words as well as create a dramatic pause or highlight a word or phrase spoken just before it. As with other aspects of cre-ative writing, the placement of a caesura is often personal preference. In your writing, you can simply use punctuation to determine pauses and stops.[136] Use commas for a pause and a dash for a slightly longer pause; use periods for a complete stop, the longest pause, or possibly a place to take a breath. Some people pause slightly at the end of lines in poetry, but a line break is not a true pause. Let's take a closer look at line breaks.

Line Breaks

Line breaks typically matter most in traditional, written poetry. But they can also make a difference in pieces you plan to recite. Along with punctuation, they can direct your performance. (See also enjambed and end-stopped lines in chapter 5.) It may seem arbitrary, but organizing your thoughts this way can really be useful, even if you only plan to speak the words out loud.

A Seed Blessing
Tender seeds, take root and grow,
take strength from earth and water's flow—

---

135. Addonizio and Laux, *The Poet's Companion*, 105.

136. In the process of scanning written poetry, a caesura is indicated by this symbol: | |

reach for sky, taste warmth of sun,
bear flower and fruit before you're done.
At harvest time, the seeds remain,
to share again life they contain.

This piece could also be written with short lines, like this:

Tender seeds
take root and grow,
take strength from earth
and water's flow—
reach for sky,
taste warmth of sun,
bear flower and fruit
before you're done.
At harvest time,
the seeds remain,
to share again
life they contain.

The second example is the same set of lines with different line breaks. Notice how the shorter lines draw your attention to certain words. Typically, words at the ends of lines are more noticeable; words at the beginnings of lines also create emphasis. Use this as a guide when deciding where to break your lines and stanzas. This may matter more when a piece is to be seen in writing rather than being chanted aloud, but another feature of short lines is that they often allow for more focus on the rhythm of a piece and can be chanted easier. You decide where to break your lines, where to breathe between phrases, and where you want a longer pause. Practice reciting the piece; remember, these tips are all about actively speaking.

Also note the sounds in this piece and the word choice. There is repetition of the "t" sound, and the word "take" is repeated as well; there is also parallel structure and some slant rhyme ("again" and "contain"). The words are specific too. Action words like "reach," "taste," and "bear" describe the goal. The sound matters, in addition to how you say the words and how you feel when saying them. Writing literary poems is somewhat different than writing spells. I like my spells to rhyme, but most of my poems do not.[137] This is your decision.

Word-Witch Practice
Creative Language

Use these exercises to get your creative wheels turning.

- Review previous pieces you've written for use of punctuation. Play with writing some sentences that become completely different (or humorous) when the punctuation is changed. Experiment with line breaks in previous pieces you've written. What changes can you make, and what effect do those changes have?

- Practice writing creative metaphors and similes. Start simple. What is the moon like? The sun? Explore the world around you—indoors and out—and write as many comparisons as you can. Avoid clichés.

- Again, looking around you both indoors and out—what can you personify? Pretend everything around you has a personality, a voice. What would these objects (or plants, animals, aspects of weather, etc.) say and do? What would the sun say to the grass? How does the flower feel about the bee?

- Play with personifying abstract qualities. For example, if Love, Power, Anxiety, Courage, etc. were people, what would they be like? What would they do and say? How would they interact with each other?

- Get creative with classic symbols. Beyond a heart or rose for love, what else can be symbolic of this emotion? Beyond using symbol, how would you describe what *love* is like? Try to describe as many abstract qualities as you can using figurative language.

---

137. There are many excellent books on the craft of poetry, but I recommend (especially if you're a beginner) *A Poetry Handbook* by Mary Oliver. Not just because she's one of my favorite poets, but because the book is simple, approachable, and filled with wisdom. Other good choices are *The Poet's Companion* by Kim Addonizio and Dorianne Laux and *In the Palm of Your Hand* by Steve Kowit.

- Make lists of common colors and see how many related descriptions and names for that color you can come up with. It's okay to consult a thesaurus or dictionary. For example, *yellow—chartreuse, goldenrod, banana, buttercup, lemon, maize; brown—sorrel, mahogany, chocolate, cocoa, beige, tan*.

- Sit outside and make lists of descriptive words and phrases for aspects of nature. Be as detailed as you can in relating what you see, and then move beyond description to what things remind you of or what their personality is like. Is the wind *forceful* or *gentle*? If it had a color, what would it be? What would its voice sound like? What does that maple tree look like, beyond being a tree or tall or green? Describe the leaves and bark. Maybe the leaves are like green paper stars and the bark is like gray wrinkled paper.

- If you find yourself using the same words over and over, make lists of synonyms you could try. For example, instead of *protect*, you could use *defend, guard,* or *shield*.

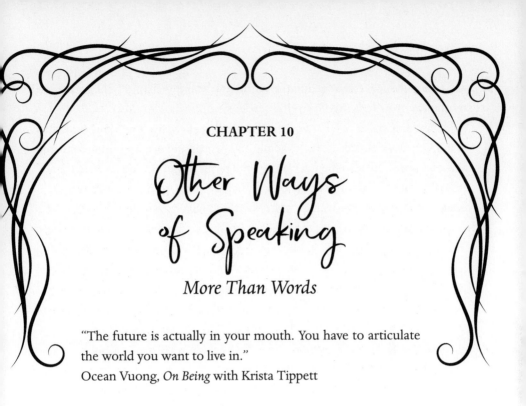

CHAPTER 10

Other Ways of Speaking

More Than Words

"The future is actually in your mouth. You have to articulate the world you want to live in."
Ocean Vuong, *On Being* with Krista Tippett

Reciting spells, affirmations, and prayers out loud can be an essential part of your magic. Even if you're a solitary practitioner, your performance counts because it affects and reflects your attitude, and this, in turn, impacts your actions. Your thoughts matter as well. Even if you're alone, some consideration should still be given to your performance. In addition, this chapter also addresses some other ways you can experiment with words and sounds.

Talking to Yourself (and Others)

We all know the power of our thoughts, the power that worry and anxiety can hold over us. Our internal conversations with ourselves shape who we are, what we believe, and how we perceive the world—and our place in it. It's often difficult to silence our internal monologue, which can contain harmful words of self-doubt. But in magical practice, it is essential that we cultivate a positive attitude. Ultimately, no magical tools are more powerful than your belief and will. Without them, your words will be empty. To make the most of your magical practice and avoid "empty words," don't think of the act as mere recitation, as something mundane or ordinary—put your intent behind each word and feel it, visualize it affecting the world and making change. The same goes for the way you "talk" to yourself.

According to Shinzen Young in *The Science of Enlightenment: How Meditation Works*, our "mental talk" consists not only of words (phrases and entire sentences and narratives) but also mental pictures and physical and emotional sensations.[138] Recognizing all these aspects of our thoughts is important because, eventually, images and specific words fade away; "at that point, you begin to detect a subtle undercurrent, a sort of subterranean stirring in image space and talk space. That's your subconscious mind!"[139] Young goes on to point out that fostering "sensitivity to how words are used in different contexts … is a benchmark of spiritual maturity."[140] We think in words, and words are important, but at some point, we move beyond them. However, awareness of words is the first step in addressing our internal conversation and our attitudes about ourselves and others.

A negative attitude about yourself or low self-esteem will destroy your magic. Cultivate positivity in whatever way you can. Try to avoid internalizing negative statements like "I can't do it" or "It's not possible." Turn those phrases around to find a positive approach. Create meaningful affirmations that you can say to yourself. You may need to do some serious reflection and self-analysis to get to the root of any negative attitudes you may have (about yourself and others). They may be so buried you don't even realize they exist. The practice of journaling can help you discover some of these feelings. Take time to record and explore your thoughts, feelings, dreams, etc. Consult a therapist or counselor. Try divination and meditation. All of these practices can help you address energy blocks that are preventing you from realizing and achieving your full potential.

It's also important to consider what we say to others. Often when we have good intentions—seeking to comfort or encourage, for example—we say things that belittle or dismiss someone's suffering. Try to avoid saying things like "It could be worse, so be thankful…" or "Don't dwell on it" or "Everything happens for a reason," or "Time heals all wounds," and the one I dislike the most: "Bloom where you're planted." I know this phrase is meant to imply that there

---

138. Shinzen Young, *The Science of Enlightenment: How Meditation Works* (Boulder, CO: Sounds True, 2016), 88, 90.

139. Young, *The Science of Enlightenment*, 89.

140. Young, *The Science of Enlightenment*, 117.

are some things that are out of a person's control, and the hard part is finding a way to make the best of a difficult situation. But what if the situation is impossible? What if you're planted in the wrong place and can't move? A plant can't dig itself up. A shade-loving plant placed in full sun cannot survive. Most of the time, people mean well; they just don't know what to say, so they fall back on common phrases that aren't really useful or helpful. Sometimes a person who's hurting just needs someone to listen. They just need to express their grief and pain—that leads to healing. Sometimes we don't even need words.

And as we all often use words to describe our identity, here is another area where words matter. Paying attention to the use of people's preferred pronouns deserves increased awareness. In addition, much attention has been given in recent years to avoiding sexist language—like saying *server* instead of *waiter* or *waitress*. For many decades, feminists have sought to reclaim the word *witch* as the wise woman archetype, but this word is not just for women—many people seek to reclaim this word as the image of a healer or person of wisdom. It's not being overly sensitive to be considerate of the words we use to describe others and ourselves—it's a sign of respect. And as the saying goes, "Watch your thoughts, they become your words; watch your words, they become your actions; watch your actions, they become your habits; watch your habits, they become your character; watch your character, it becomes your destiny."[141]

Speaking of speaking, we don't just talk to other people. We talk to our pets and even our plants. I mention this because there is compelling evidence that "talking" to plants (and other nonhuman beings) is beneficial, and this reinforces the magic of words and sound. The simple act of articulating our thoughts and feelings can have a therapeutic effect, helping us be more mindful.[142] Whether or not you believe that plants respond to our voices, the fact is that sound is a vibration, and vibrations (sound waves) travel and encounter other things. From a magical standpoint, if you believe your words and intent are making change, then it's happening on some level. (For more on vibrations, see chapter 17, Words and Numbers.)

---

141. Attributed to a variety of authors and philosophers; no one is actually certain where this statement originated.

142. Stacey Colino, "The Case for Talking to Your Houseplants," *Washington Post*, January 11, 2023, *Gale OneFile: Business* (accessed October 23, 2023), np, https://www.washingtonpost.com/home/2023/01/11/talking-to-plants-grow-thrive/.

When I was in sixth grade, I did an experiment for the school science fair to see if music would affect the growth of plants—in this case, bean sprouts. Not groundbreaking work, of course, but fun for a kid. The plants exposed to classical music grew faster and larger than the other two groups (one without music, and one with rock music). I received a ribbon for my work, but I don't recall what ultimately happened to the plants. The topic of music, spirituality, and our brains is an entirely different discussion, but on the subject of words and magic, it's just more evidence that the things we say, the sounds we make, are an important part of our lives, our world, and our magic.

It's worth taking time to reflect on the words you use every day (in speech and thought) to see if you're drawing negativity without realizing it. Continuously focusing on your perceived flaws, for example, can lower your self-esteem over time. It's also important to consider how you respond to others. If you truly want your magical practice to be part of your life, you need to consider how it impacts everything you do and how what you say (and do) reflects your true self.

Mantras

While we're on the topic of sounds, we need to give some consideration to mantras. While I'm no expert on Eastern traditions, I have spent a great deal of time studying meditation and the use of mantras. A *mantra* can be a word, phrase, or sound (or series of sounds), but whatever you choose needs to have meaning for you. If this is of interest to you, I urge you to study and learn as much as you can from experts in this area. However, there are some valuable concepts that also apply to magic that you can use right away. According to *The Ancient Science of Mantras,* the serious student of mantra first understands the essential concept that the words, phrases, and sounds draw the attention of universal energy toward us. The goal is "to practice the utterance of a sound with such intensity, fervor and determination, that your whole being starts to reverberate with that sound. You become that sound. It becomes your sound, your mantra. The one you not only connect with, but that transports you to another dimension of consciousness."[143]

---

143. Om Swami, *The Ancient Science of Mantras: Wisdom of the Sages* (India: Black Lotus Press, 2017), Kindle.

But remember, the mantra you choose needs to have meaning for you. You can write your own or do some research to find one. In chapter 11, we will explore the concept of key words and the One-Word Spell. A key word can definitely be used as a mantra. Think of a mantra as a type of affirmation but with a deeper spiritual resonance. Choose a word, short phrase, or sound that has a deep meaning for you. Rather than just repeating it whenever you feel the need, the speaking of a mantra should ideally be done in a meditative state or, at the very least, when you can give the act your full attention. While affirmations can be spoken while doing other things (shopping, driving, exercising), a mantra should be something you can engage with while being still and fully present in the act. When you chant a mantra, it must be an emotional expression—quality over quantity. Chanting a thousand times won't be effective without feeling. Your personal expression is crucial—your faith in the mantra and your spiritual path. It's very much like the act of meditation—it works best when you are fully committed. You can chant out loud or silently to yourself.

Again returning to the advice from *The Ancient Science of Mantras*, there are four types of chanting used for mantras: spoken, whispered, mental, and unspoken. Spoken is obvious—you speak out loud in an audible fashion where even other people could hear you. Speaking words out loud serves the function of increasing the connection of our internal world to the external. Whispering is nearly inaudible speech; you move your lips but make very little sound—this leads to increased concentration. Mental chanting is solely in the mind. According to Om Swami, "whispered chanting is better than spoken chanting…and mental [chanting] is ten times more effective," allowing even more focus on the energy of your mantra.[144] Eventually, you can move to the ultimate stage: unspoken chanting. This is where the chanting is no longer an act of consciousness. The mantra becomes part of you, and it happens to you naturally—like a running commentary in the back of your mind. At this level, you transcend the boundary between the conscious and unconscious mind. This takes an immense amount of practice. But the point is, basically, "the softer you chant your mantra, the closer you get to the source."[145]

---

144. Om Swami, *The Ancient Science of Mantras*.

145. Om Swami, *The Ancient Science of Mantras*.

It's important to consider what you believe to be the "source." What is the source of your spirituality? Name it, if you can—remember, names have power. Is it the Universe? Your higher self? Is it a deity or pantheon of deities? Nature? Remember, you are intimately connected to this source. Removing obstacles between the surface and the "source" is a path to enlightenment.[146] During meditation, you ultimately discover that you are not merely yourself—body and mind—but you are, actually, the source of your mind and body, which is also the source of all minds and all bodies. This is a profound part of the spiritual journey.

These techniques for chanting mantras can assist you with all forms of magical practice. Repetition of words and phrases is a significant part of magic and always has been; strengthening the mind and the will is essential to the process. Approach the activity with mindfulness and total devotion to your goal, but don't worry if it takes time and practice. It's all part of the journey. Given that meditation and altered states of consciousness are the foundation skills of magical practice, you can use your chosen mantra for this purpose.

Words and Chakras

Building on the use of mantras, you can apply that technique to working with the chakras. The seven major chakras are the energy centers of our body, imagined as spinning wheels—a concept from India that dates back to 1500 to 1000 BCE, first mentioned in the sacred teachings from the Vedas. While there are particular chakras we can associate with speaking and the voice, you can use any of these energy centers to aid your visualization. Remember, the breath is associated with your voice, sounds, and language, and connects you with the Universal or Divine Consciousness. Visualize an energy flow, network, web, or chain that can manifest your words.

You can visualize your words coming *from* a particular chakra or going *to* that area if you need to clear a blockage. Here's an example: Let's say you're working magic to draw love into your life. As you speak the words of your spell, put one hand on your chest (corresponding to the heart chakra) and hold your other hand out, either palm up or whatever feels right to you. Visualize the words of your spell coming from your heart—your emotional center—

---

146. Young, *The Science of Enlightenment*, 184.

or flowing into it or both. For healing magic, put one hand (or both) on the related area(s) of the body and visualize your words drawing energy to those places. Using the list provided below, choose other aspects of that chakra to accompany your spell. You could play music associated with that particular chakra, chant a mantra, use colors, etc.

Associations with each chakra also include sounds and particular syllables you can chant, as well as sounds made by particular instruments that correspond to each. The "a" sound in each is typically the "ah" or "uh" sound. There's really no wrong way to do this. However, you can find videos online if you want to hear some examples. Additionally, you can chant the key words or phrases associated with a specific chakra as you would chant a mantra, or create your own mantra. We often meditate on images or just clear our minds, but we can also focus our attention on a specific word or phrase. Sustained focus on a word or phrase as meditation is often part of chakra work and can be used in magical practice as well.

The following table presents some aspects of each chakra.

Chakra Correspondences

Root: *Muladhara* means "root support." This chakra, the first chakra, is associated with being comfortable with yourself—being grounded, feeling secure, healthy, and present in the moment.

- Location: base of the spine and tailbone area
- Purpose: grounding, foundation, survival and self-preservation
- Influences: stability and grounding, support, nourishment and security
- Color: red
- Sense: smell
- Element: Earth
- Mantra: *Lam* / "I am"
- Instrument: drums

Sacral: *Svadisthana* means "one's own place." The second chakra governs nurturing (others and yourself), your ability to accept change and be in control of your emotions, setting boundaries, and enjoying pleasure.

- Location: lower abdomen, just below belly button
- Purpose: movement, flow
- Influences: emotions, pleasure and sexuality, creativity
- Color: orange
- Sense: taste
- Element: Water
- Mantra: *Vam* / "I feel"
- Instruments: flute and woodwinds

Solar plexus: *Manipura* means "lustrous gem." The third chakra is associated with strength of will and intent—your ability to use action to reach your goals and desires.

- Location: upper abdomen
- Purpose: energy and will
- Influences: confidence and self-esteem, personal power, individuation
- Color: yellow
- Sense: sight
- Element: Fire
- Mantra: *Ram* / "I do"
- Instrument: organ

Heart: *Anahata* means "unstruck" or "unhurt." The fourth chakra concerns all aspects of caring and being empathetic; it also governs being content and the ability to find inner peace.

- Location: center of the chest
- Purpose: compassion, love
- Influences: relationships, balance, self-love
- Color: green

- Sense: touch
- Element: Air
- Mantra: *Yam* / "I love"
- Instruments: violin and string instruments

Throat: *Vishuddha* means "purification." The fifth chakra concerns good communication at all levels (speaking and listening). Due to its association with the throat, it also literally involves making sounds and expressing yourself in this way.

- Location: throat
- Purpose: communication, creativity
- Influence: self-expression (and listening to others)
- Color: blue
- Sense: hearing
- Element: Ether
- Mantra: *Ham* / "I speak"
- Instruments: horns

Third Eye: *Ajna* means both to "perceive" and to "command." The sixth chakra is the source of your inner light and insight. Other aspects of this chakra include memory, dreaming, and visualization skills.

- Location: forehead, between the eyes
- Purpose: intuition and insight, seeing
- Influences: clarity, vision, and imagination
- Color: indigo
- Sense: intuition
- Element: Light (transcendence)
- Mantra: *Om* or *Aum* / "I see"[147]
- Instrument: piano

---

147. *Om* is a mantra associated with both the third eye and crown chakras. Some schools of thought contend that these alternate spellings indicate that Aum is simply the extended sound of Om, created by emphasizing each part of the sound (spending more time on the "a," "u," and "m") and that both are appropriate. However, a difference for each chakra can be established by chanting the mantra aloud for the third eye chakra and chanting silently for the crown chakra.

Crown: *Sahasrara* means "thousand-fold." The seventh chakra is associated with Divine Consciousness, wisdom, and enlightenment—the realization that you are one with the Divine. In addition, critical thinking skills, analysis, and being open-minded are also aspects of this chakra.

- Location: top of the head
- Purpose: pure awareness, unity with Divine, understanding
- Influences: spiritual connections, intelligence
- Color: violet or white
- Sense: withdrawal of senses
- Elements: thought and consciousness
- Mantra: *Om* or *Aum* (chanted silently) / "I know"
- Instrument: conch shell

Mumbo Jumbo—Mysterious Words

Scholars have noted that in ancient times, it didn't matter if someone understood the actual words as long as there was belief in their efficacy. Latin was the liturgical language from the Middle Ages through the nineteenth century, and it was also the language of magic. It's worth noting that "people who attended sermons given in this language often did not understand a word of them," and, in fact, strange sounds strengthened the magical experience.[148] Have you ever been captivated by music sung in a foreign language just because of the feelings it evoked, even if you couldn't understand a word? That mystery can be very appealing. Nonsense words have the same effect and can be made of random sounds or be words that you invent for a special purpose.

If you'd like to use words from Latin or another language because you like the way they sound, do it! But it can also be fun to invent your own words for things (see chapter 18). You can combine words or be inspired by words that sound like what they are. The made-up word *"lumos"* sounds like "light" or "illuminate," but it's not a real word.[149] *Lumen* means "light" in Latin. You can

---

148. Claude Lecouteux, *Dictionary of Ancient Magic Words and Spells from Abraxas to Zoar* (Rochester: Inner Traditions, 2014) loc. 270; 344, Kindle.

149. J. K. Rowling, *Harry Potter and the Chamber of Secrets* (New York: Arthur A. Levine Books, 1999), 272.

come up with your own words for things or borrow. Or create combinations of sounds that resonate with you.

And then there's onomatopoeia. Most people are familiar with this technique—words that sound like, well, sounds. *Bam! Pff! Whoosh! Hiss. Buzz. Thump.* Making sounds that aren't actually words can be a useful part of magic. You can mimic sounds in nature, such as wind or water, make tapping sounds, rattle, etc. These are all ways we can alter our consciousness.

On a side note, while the phrase *mumbo jumbo* is intended to be humorous and suggest the use of words or language that is incomprehensible (intentionally or otherwise), the phrase is not meaningless. It's actually from West Africa and refers to a type of masked spiritual dancer called a "Maamajomboo."[150] There are other cited examples of possible meanings as well. So when you're choosing a word, do a little research in case it really does mean something to someone else. Use online etymology dictionaries to dig into the origins and evolution of words.

Singing

While it's not in the scope of this book to discuss music in depth, certainly you can see how that plays an important role in magic. Chanting can become singing, and sometimes just making a particular sound is enough. We often see that the particular terms used to describe "witches' spells and charms are frequently based on words having to do with song (or the noise and sound by which incantations are produced)."[151] The root word of *charm* is the Latin *carmen*, which means "song," and even the word *incantation* contains *cantare*, Latin, "to sing." Etymologically speaking, the English word *sing* in its various forms comes from a Proto-Indo-European root **sengwh-* "to sing, make an incantation."[152]

150. Lakshmi Gandhi, "Unmasking the Meaning and Marital Disputes behind Mumbo Jumbo," NPR, May 31, 2014, https://www.npr.org/sections/codeswitch/2014/05/31/317442320/unmasking-the-meaning-and-marital-disputes-behind-mumbo-jumbo.

151. Stephen A. Mitchell, *Witchcraft and Magic in the Nordic Middle Ages* (Philadelphia, PA: University of Pennsylvania Press, 2011), Kindle.

152. "Charm," Etymology Online, accessed May 20, 2024, https://www.etymonline.com/word/charm#etymonline_v_8449; "Incantation," Merriam-Webster, accessed May 20, 2024, https://www.merriam-webster.com/dictionary/incantation; "Sing," Etymology Online, accessed July 28, 2023, https://www.etymonline.com/word/sing#etymonline_v_23556.

This is worth noting because singing has so often been an expression of spirituality and magic.

Research has shown how listening to singing engages different parts of the brain than other sounds, including instrumental music. There's something special about the music of the human voice.[153] But the act of singing (and actively participating in musical performance) has been shown to have positive effects on the body and emotions. It triggers the "happy" hormonal secretions (endorphins, dopamine, serotonin, and oxytocin), increases oxygen levels in your blood, strengthens lung function, improves memory, and can even help relieve anxiety and pain.[154]

Even if you can't carry a tune, try it anyway. Do it when you're comfortably alone so you're not self-conscious about it. There's a reason why so many of us love singing in the car or in the shower!

Word-Witch Practice
Other Ways of Speaking

Use these activities to explore how you speak in your magical practice.

- Write down as much of your "internal talk" as you can. What thoughts do you dwell on the most? Which negative ones can you replace with something positive?

- Make a list of words and phrases you could use as a mantra. Brainstorm these in your journal, and write down the goal of each one.

- Invent your own nonsense words. Could you use some of these in your magical practice? For more on creating words, see chapter 18.

- Practice visualization techniques that correspond with your words; meditate on the specific chakras or parts of the body where the sounds and words originate.

153. Anne Trafton, "Singing in the Brain," MIT News, February 22, 2022, https://news.mit.edu/2022/singing-neurons-0222.

154. Rebecca Joy Stanborough, "10 Ways That Singing Benefits Your Health," Healthline, November 10, 2020, https://www.healthline.com/health/benefits-of-singing.

- Practice singing some of the chants you've written. If you can't come up with a melody, just use something familiar (like "Twinkle, Twinkle, Little Star") or a popular song you enjoy as a starting point. Alternately, take a melody you like from popular music and write a chant using that tune.

- Sing along with recorded music and chants if you aren't comfortable singing on your own. It has the same effect. Once you've memorized a recorded piece, try it on your own, without the recording. The more you practice, the more comfortable and confident you will become.

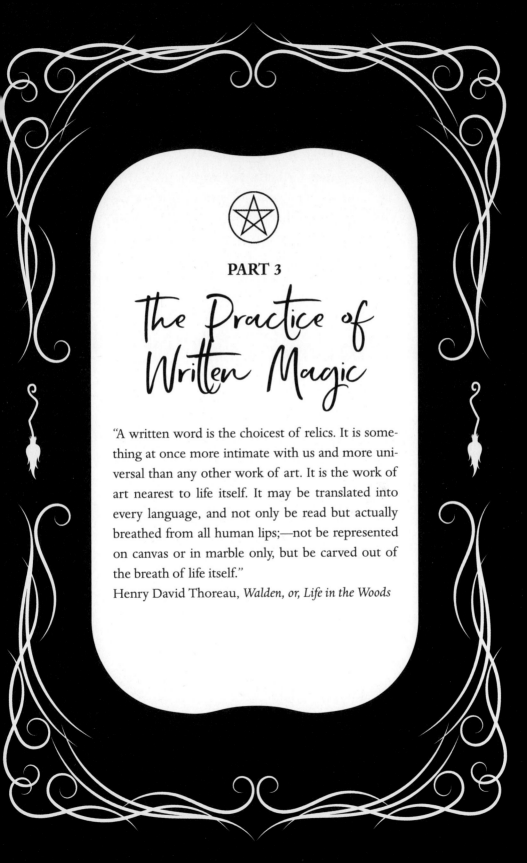

PART 3

The Practice of Written Magic

"A written word is the choicest of relics. It is something at once more intimate with us and more universal than any other work of art. It is the work of art nearest to life itself. It may be translated into every language, and not only be read but actually breathed from all human lips;—not be represented on canvas or in marble only, but be carved out of the breath of life itself."

Henry David Thoreau, *Walden, or, Life in the Woods*

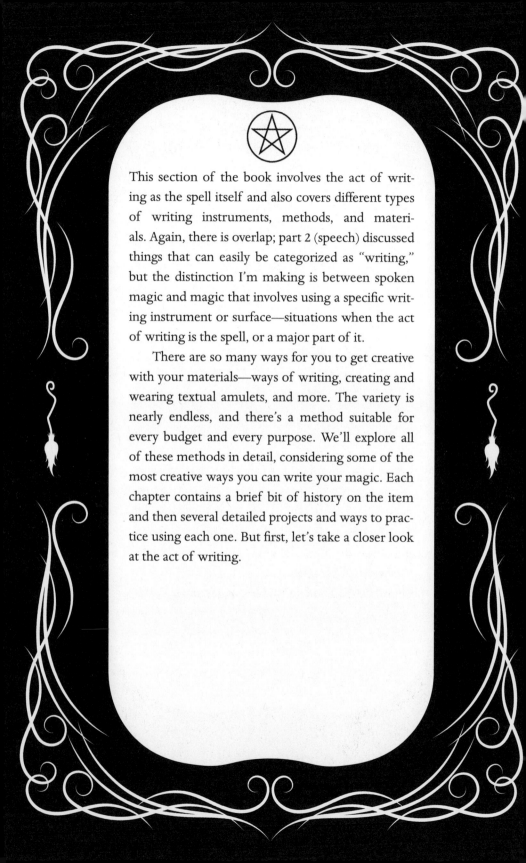

This section of the book involves the act of writing as the spell itself and also covers different types of writing instruments, methods, and materials. Again, there is overlap; part 2 (speech) discussed things that can easily be categorized as "writing," but the distinction I'm making is between spoken magic and magic that involves using a specific writing instrument or surface—situations when the act of writing is the spell, or a major part of it.

There are so many ways for you to get creative with your materials—ways of writing, creating and wearing textual amulets, and more. The variety is nearly endless, and there's a method suitable for every budget and every purpose. We'll explore all of these methods in detail, considering some of the most creative ways you can write your magic. Each chapter contains a brief bit of history on the item and then several detailed projects and ways to practice using each one. But first, let's take a closer look at the act of writing.

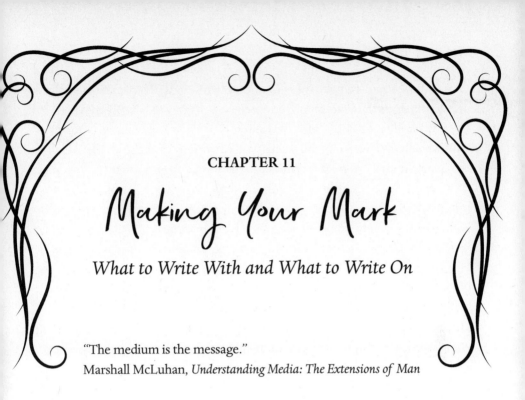

CHAPTER 11

Making Your Mark

What to Write With and What to Write On

"The medium is the message."
Marshall McLuhan, *Understanding Media: The Extensions of Man*

Writing developed alongside the materials used to deliver the messages. From carving and painting on stone and clay, to wax and wood tablets, to parchment, papyrus, and paper, there has always been a relationship between the content and the context. The development of various mediums has changed the way the messages were created; as civilizations grew and developed new technologies, not only did the materials of communication change, these changes affected (and still affect) the messages themselves.[155]

When seeking the appropriate materials for your purpose, choosing materials for your written magic can enhance your spell and will largely be determined by your goal. There are many things to consider. Will your spell be something visible or hidden? Or hidden in plain sight? Will it be permanent or consumed in some way? Which Elements will you employ? Is your goal projective or receptive; are you drawing something to you or trying to send something away? Is the magic for someone else? Is the end result the goal, such as creating a magical object or amulet, or is the action itself the main goal? Do you need to destroy the item as part of the spell—dispose of it in some way?

---

155. Zender, *Writing and Civilization*, 187.

Or will this be something to carry or display? These are all factors that help you decide which method is best for your spell (see chapter 20, The Elements).

For basic text-based spells, obviously, your choice of what to write *with* will partially be determined by what you're writing *on*. First decide which is most important to you—the material to mark on, or the implement you want to write with. Choose the "ink" or the "surface"—whichever you choose first will determine the other. If you want to use chalk, for example, you will be somewhat limited by the type of surface you can write on. The same goes for writing on your skin. There are temporary tattoo pens if you don't want it to be permanent. You can also write on your skin with lip liner or eyeliner (see chapter 15).

This choice may seem like an overwhelming decision, given that there are so many options—pens, markers, pencils and colored pencils, crayons, paint, chalk, and more. Even nonconventional things can be used to write—lipstick, nail polish, ash and charcoal, fruit juice, blood—basically anything that can leave a mark. You can write on stones, shells, and other natural items like leaves or tree bark. Experiment with which type of writing works best on the particular surface. To write on a leaf, a ballpoint pen works well. You can try other things, like markers, too. For wood, use a marker, pencil, or paint—it depends on the wood and whether you're using a piece of bark, a flat piece of wood, or one that's rough or smooth.

The Magic of Writing

Handwriting is an important skill that has many benefits. Studies have shown that the brain is more active during handwriting than typing on a keyboard. Writing can aid memory as well.[156] As a writer, I use a combination of writing by hand and typing when I create, even when I'm writing something that will ultimately be spoken magic. But when the act of writing is part of the spell itself, particular attention should be paid to what you're writing with, what material you're writing on, and the way you focus on the words.

---

156. Eva Ose Askvik, F. R. (Ruud) van der Weel, and Audrey L. H. van der Meer, "The Importance of Cursive Handwriting over Typewriting for Learning in the Classroom: A High-Density EEG Study of 12-Year-Old Children and Young Adults," *Frontiers in Psychology* 11 (July 2020), https://www.frontiersin .org/journals/psychology/articles/10.3389/fpsyg.2020.01810/full.

Sometimes in our magical practice, we become so concerned with the herbs or crystals, the timing, or the color of the candle that we forget the power of the words themselves; they are conduits for our will and intent.[157] And as with all other aspects of magical practice, visualization is essential. As you write, "imagine that the surface of the paper [or other material] represents Universal Consciousness and the ink [or other substance] represents your unconscious."[158] In this case, writing is a way to make a connection between our personal consciousness and the Divine or Universal Consciousness. The point is that every time you speak or write during magical practice, you consider the power of the words as a type of communication—either divine or as a way of the universal life force being expressed. You are writing (or speaking) your will into existence.

When writing or carving the words of a spell, take care in shaping each letter and word. Stay focused on your goal during the entire process. Visualize your intent flowing from your hand into the writing instrument and into the object. See the words themselves being activated with magic—this is an act of creation. Your energy is being used and projected. It can be released in the writing itself or when the piece you've made is being buried, burned, etc. This is very important to the process.

Print, Cursive, or Type?

Throughout history, having good penmanship was considered a mark of high status. The ancient Romans created an elaborate script, but in the late eighth century, Charlemagne instructed an English monk to standardize it. Centuries later, even though the printing press made block-style characters popular, some Italians resisted the change, preferring the elegant script (this is where we get the term *italic*) and created an even more elaborate style of writing.[159] Fast-forward to the mid-1800s when a teacher invented a more practical style of writing (referred to

157. It's worth noting that not every culture gives words the same emphasis we do, given our traditions based on European practices.

158. Dean Radin, *Real Magic: Ancient Wisdom, Modern Science, and a Guide to the Secret Power of the Universe* (New York: Harmony Books, 2018), Kindle.

159. Jennie Cohen, "A Brief History of Penmanship on National Handwriting Day," History, updated May 16, 2023, https://www.history.com/news/a-brief-history-of-penmanship-on-national-handwriting-day.

as Spencerian penmanship), which was changed yet again to make it faster, resulting in the Palmer Method that would probably look familiar to most of us.[160]

I remember having to learn cursive writing in elementary school, and while some kids probably thought it was a chore, I loved it. Today many schools are no longer teaching cursive writing, but there's a trend to add it back into the curriculum, which is good news.[161] Studies have shown that any type of writing aids memory, but cursive is better at helping develop fine motor skills.[162] Cursive was developed with the goal of making writing faster, but evidence shows that it really doesn't. In fact, many of us employ a method of combining print with cursive script—this is called D'Nealian style.[163]

While print and cursive both have merits, the choice is yours, as always. Your magical writing will most likely depend on the writing surface or implement you're using—or even your mood. Printing letters slowly and deliberately can create a focused approach; cursive writing has an elegant appeal. There are benefits to both styles.

Having said that, what about typing your spells? I love creating documents with pretty fonts and other embellishments. There's a place for that in magic too. You can create beautiful documents using a combination of techniques—typing and printing using a computer, adding images, and more. Creating this way should not be considered inferior. Each method has its merits.

Word-Witch Practice
The One-Word Spell

Many parts of this book overlap regarding spoken and written magic—especially if you're only using one word. But don't dismiss one-word spells as sim-

160. Beth Gottschling Huber, "Don't Write Off Cursive Yet," National Museum of American History. February 24, 2022, https://americanhistory.si.edu/explore/stories/dont-write-cursive-yet.

161. Gottschling, "Don't Write Off Cursive Yet."

162. Christopher Bergland, "4 Reasons Writing Things Down on Paper Still Reigns Supreme," Psychology Today, March 19, 2021, https://www.psychologytoday.com/us/blog/the-athletes-way/202103/4-reasons-writing-things-down-paper-still-reigns-supreme; Jimmy McTiernan, "Is it Faster to Write in Cursive or Print?" The Productive Engineer, updated July 27, 2021, https://theproductiveengineer.net/is-it-faster-to-write-in-cursive-or-print.

163. McTiernan, "Is it Faster to Write in Cursive or Print?"

ple. Spells that involve the writing or speaking of a single word can be just as powerful as an elaborate chant. I'm mentioning this type of magic here because one-word spells can be of particular use in written magic when the act of writing or carving the word onto a specific surface (or the use of other materials) is a significant part of the spell. For example, key words might be things like *love, healing, strength, calm, forgive/forgiveness, justice, protect/protection, success, wealth, abundance, joy*—something you want to draw to you or a quality you want to possess or manifest. Or if you want to use a key word you intend to destroy, then choose the name of that thing you wish to be rid of. For example, *guilt, grief, anger, jealousy*, etc.

First, consider word choice. Begin by brainstorming words that are associated with your specific intent. Just make a list of words. Consult a thesaurus if you wish. Then choose the best word for your purpose—one that resonates with you and one that you feel really expresses, in just one word, the totality of your purpose and goal. Remember, your visualization will also support your magical intent.

Next, consider action. This part of the spell is determined by your goal. Are you drawing something to you or sending it away? Do you want to create an amulet or talisman you can carry or wear? Is the act of writing or carving the word important? For example, you can write the word on an object, such as paper, your body, etc., or make it invisible. You can carve it into wood or clay and carry the word with you, display it, destroy it—whatever feels most appropriate (see chapter 20, The Elements, for more ideas).

Here's an example: Let's say you want to banish someone from your life who is causing you distress. Words that come to mind would be *banish*, of course, but other good choices are *leave, move, depart, disappear*, etc. You may find it hard to choose one word, but that's the power of this spell. Choose your word with care. There are differences between words like *leave* and *disappear*, for example. That one word that you shout, whisper, chant, write, burn, or bury is the focus of all your energy and intent. Think of it like a seed—a tiny acorn that will eventually become a towering oak, or a stone thrown into a pond that makes the water ripple outward over and over again until it reaches the shore. This is something that starts small but grows and grows in power, eventually having a huge impact—a shout that echoes.

The One-Word Spell can be a powerful chant or mantra (see chapters 5, 6, and 10). Be sure the visualization (and other actions, if used) accompanying the spell is very specific. Whether you write or speak, be sure you have a clear mental image of your goal. In addition, choosing one key word to represent your goal means giving careful consideration to word choice. If you're speaking one word, be sure the word you've chosen to say doesn't sound like something else.

Word play is fun, but homonyms can cause confusion (depending on whether you're writing or speaking). There are two types of homonyms. *Homophones* sound the same but have a different spelling—*heir* and *air*, or *to, too,* and *two. Homographs* are spelled the same but differ in meaning or pronunciation—*bow* (as it pertains to a ship or the act of bending over) and *bow* (as a ribbon); *minute* (a unit of time) and *minute* (very tiny); *wind* (as in wrapping something) and *wind* (air flow). Keep this in mind when choosing your words.

Ultimately, the One-Word Spell offers a great deal of creative freedom for using words as the focus of your magic. Don't underestimate this power.

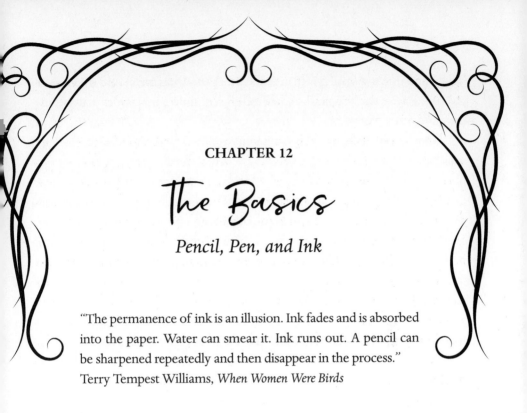

CHAPTER 12

The Basics

Pencil, Pen, and Ink

"The permanence of ink is an illusion. Ink fades and is absorbed
into the paper. Water can smear it. Ink runs out. A pencil can
be sharpened repeatedly and then disappear in the process."
Terry Tempest Williams, *When Women Were Birds*

This chapter will explore some of the simplest ways to write: pen and pencil.
While this may seem boring or basic, there is actually quite a bit of variety
here, and these simple writing instruments can be more magical than you may
have imagined.

The Pencil

The simple pencil is the tool of choice for architects and artists. The origin
of the name can be seen in the Latin *penicillium*, which means "fine brush"
and the Old French *pincel*, which means "'paintbrush.'"[164] The pencil as we
know it today was developed more than five hundred years ago. A fallen tree
in England exposed what was first thought to be metal but turned out to be
graphite—pure carbon. (Graphite comes from the Greek *graphein*, which
means "to write.") Of course, they didn't call it that at the time. It performed
better than lead (which was used previously) to make marks on paper, so they
just called it *black lead*. Sticks were formed of this material, wrapped in paper or

---

164. Zender, *Writing and Civilization*, 182.

string, and used as writing instruments. The pencil was born! And the remarkable thing was that the marks could be erased, unlike ink, which was permanent and often messy.

Somewhere along the line, someone came up with the idea of placing a stick of graphite inside wood, which created a sturdier writing tool. As supplies of graphite became scarce, an inventive French scientist, Nicolas-Jacques Conté, found a way to blend it with clay and then encase it in wood. This pencil design was patented in 1795 and eventually became the most popular style.

Before the invention of the eraser, breadcrumbs were used to remove the marks. In 1858, an American named Hymen Lipman was the first person to attach an eraser to the top of a pencil.[165] In 1915 the mechanical pencil was perfected in Japan. The pencil has come a long way since then, with myriad colors and different levels of hardness, but you can still find the rectangular carpenter's pencil, which closely resembles the first ones that were made.

Don't dismiss the elegance of a fine pencil, and don't discount them for their impermanence. As the epigraph of this chapter points out, writing is, in fact, ephemeral. We think of the written word as somehow permanent, at least when compared to the spoken word, but it's as impermanent as most human creations. Even when carved in stone, it can be worn away.

The Pen

The origins of the word *pen* are rooted in the Old French word *penne*, or "quill pen." And "in turn, the French word came from Classical Latin *penna*, which meant 'feather.'"[166] Quill pens made of large feathers were common beginning in the seventh century.

There is evidence that split-nib (a *nib* is the writing tip) writing instruments existed in the Middle Ages with nibs made from a variety of materials—everything from wood and bone to eventually metal—and were used alongside quills. The use of metal-nib pens dipped into ink became widespread in the early nineteenth century. One advantage of dipping a pen into ink is that there's little concern over the ink reservoir becoming clogged, allowing for many different types of inks and other pigments to be used. This is one reason dip pens

---

165. Jonathan Schifman, "The Write Stuff: How the Humble Pencil Conquered the World," *Popular Mechanics*, August 16, 2016, https://www.popularmechanics.com/technology/a21567/history-of-the-pencil/.

166. Zender, *Writing and Civilization*, 182.

are still favored by some modern artists. But over time, a desire increased for a pen with a reservoir that could hold ink. Creation of such an instrument was attempted many times and evolved throughout the world, beginning in Europe in the seventeenth century, until, eventually, the fountain pen was perfected. Mass-produced fountain pens became available in the 1880s, and they've continued to evolve.

For casual writing, it's hard to beat the ballpoint pen, developed in the late nineteenth century. What we commonly call "felt-tip" pens (pens with soft tips) started to be used in the 1960s. However, in the world of writing implements, my favorite is the fountain pen.

I started collecting fountain pens a few years ago. You can buy a simple, good-quality fountain pen for around twenty dollars or less. Nibs come in different sizes and styles, so you can write with a very fine point or a thick one. Regarding the ink, you also have many options—buying ink refill cartridges or buying bottles of ink and using those to fill the pens. I like doing both. Not all pens have both options, but most of them do. Do your research and experiment; read reviews and articles. There really is a fountain pen for every budget.

For magical work, it's nice to have some designated writing instruments that you only use for the purpose of writing spells—even if it's just an ordinary pen that you've charged for magical use. However, if you want something more special, consider buying a refillable pen (they're better for the environment anyway) and dedicate it to your Craft. A simple ballpoint pen is low maintenance, and you can change the ink color with the replacement cartridges.

I have a ballpoint pen hand-carved from wood in its own wooden box that I received as a college graduation gift. While I love using fountain pens, this simple ballpoint pen is perfect for most magical writing. It works well on surfaces where a fountain pen isn't always suitable. It has replaceable ink cartridges, so I can charge those for magical use as well.

Disposable pens and markers come in a variety of colors and are fun to use, but consider the environmental impact of discarding the empty container. This is one reason bottles of ink and fountain pens are so appealing—you don't have numerous pen casings or ink cartridges to throw away (and you can recycle the ink bottles).

As with any hobby, you can take this as far as your passion carries you or just keep it simple. Even just having a special, dedicated pen that you use only for magic can be very rewarding.

Project
Make a Quill Pen

Historically, the quill has been one of the most popular methods of writing. Quills were fashioned from the flight feathers of large birds; the shaft was cut and dipped into ink. Writing with a quill, which has a tip more flexible than a steel nib, allows for more artistic freedom, which has kept their popularity alive. When I was a kid, my dad taught me to make "cheater" quill pens by simply inserting a ballpoint ink pen refill cartridge into the hollow shaft of a feather. If you want to write with a feather, that's a quick way to make a quill. Another alternative is to purchase a metal nib for fountain pens and attach that to the quill. But making a more authentic quill pen really isn't that hard.

Materials
- feather from large bird such as a turkey or goose
- sharp knife

Depending on the shape of the feather, you may need to strip some of the fibers from the shaft so it will be easier to hold. Using the knife (be careful!), slice off a portion of the tip diagonally and clean out the inside of the shaft (if necessary). Then cut across the tip to make it flat, and then cut a slit, like the nib of a fountain pen. The next few cuts are to shape the tip into a point. Basically, you're trying to replicate the nib of a fountain pen. Feather shafts are harder than you might think, so be sure your knife is sharp. Also, the larger the feather, the better. If you have a perfect feather, don't use it for your first try—use a practice one first.

This illustration shows the six cuts you'll need to make to create the tip.

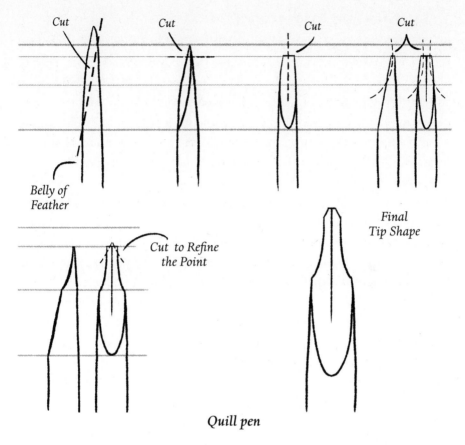

Cut   Cut   Cut   Cut

Belly of
Feather

Cut to Refine
the Point

Final
Tip Shape

Quill pen

There are many helpful videos online to guide you in creating the shape of the tip. My favorite one is at stormthecastle.com. They also have tutorials for making ink.

I've made a few feather quill pens using large goose feathers, and I can say from experience that practice makes a difference. Notice I didn't say "perfect." While I still haven't ended up with what I'd call a perfect tip, they are functional, and I can write with them. They aren't really suitable for writing anything of great length, but to write a few words or a short sentence, they work fine. It's very satisfying to write with a homemade quill pen on handmade paper using ink you've also made. I don't do this all the time; often only one of these components is handmade—the paper, the ink, or the pen—but when they all are, it's an experience to savor!

Ink

At one time, "the very act of writing itself was imbued with occult or hidden power" and certain words were believed to have power on their own, a power that could be "stimulated by the ritual use of specific inks and blood."[167] In ancient Egypt, "writing on papyrus required the use of inks, and this led to new magical notions based on their constituents. Ink containing myrrh, a resinous plant sap, was specified for some charms, for instance, and blood was sometimes intermingled," and ink was often consecrated by a priest.[168]

Historically, ink has been made from a variety of substances. While ancient humans used colored substances to make marks, the Egyptians and the Chinese can be credited with the invention of what we think of today as ink, beginning as far back as 2500 BCE. In one method, the burnt bones of animals were mixed with tar and then applied to parchment using needles. The ancient Romans developed a type of ink that used ground iron mixed with the tannin from plants—a metallic iron-gall combination.[169] At the basic level, inks are a pigment (the earliest ones were from ash or plant materials) combined with a carrier substance. In the past, animal fats were used, but today the carrier is usually water or oil. As with the development of the pen, ink has evolved as well.

Depending on your choice of writing instrument, you can buy bottled ink or cartridges. You can even purchase special inks that glow in black light. Or, if you want to be really creative, make your own ink.

Project
Blackberry Ink

The simplest homemade ink uses berries. Blackberries especially produce a very nice dark-red color. Here's how to do it on a small scale.

---

167. Davies, *Grimoires*.

168. Davies, *Grimoires*.

169. Mirta Sibilia et al., "A Multidisciplinary Study Unveils the Nature of a Roman Ink of the I Century AD," *Scientific Reports* 11, no 7231 (March 31, 2021), https://doi.org/10.1038/s41598-021-86288-x.

Materials

- 1 cup fresh blackberries or raspberries
- 1 teaspoon white vinegar
- 1 teaspoon salt

Press the berries through a strainer into a small dish. Add the white vinegar and salt and mix well. Store the ink in a sealed container, but use it quickly. If the pigment isn't dark enough, you can add a few drops of food coloring.

If you don't have a full cup of berries or just want to make enough ink for a couple projects, you can make a tiny batch. This is the method I mainly use because I like to gather the fresh wild berries that grow on my property; I usually just pick a handful to use for ink (mainly because I want to eat the rest of them!). If you only have a few berries, then just add a dash of salt and splash of vinegar to the mixture. A tiny batch like this still gives you enough ink to write quite a bit.

The vinegar helps the ink retain its color, and the salt keeps it from going rancid. Of course, if you just want to write with juice and not store the ink, you can. If your berry juice mixture is too thick, you can add a bit of water. This type of ink works great on both plain, smooth paper and handmade paper that could have a rough texture. Remember to let the ink dry fully before working with the paper (folding it, etc.).

Project
Invisible Ink

To create "invisible" ink that can only be read when heated, just about any citrus fruit juice will work. Try juice from lemons, oranges, or grapefruit. You can also try using the juice from onions. For best results, use a fine paintbrush to create the words. The paper matters too. Avoid high-quality printer paper; find something soft and uncoated. To reveal the words, use very gentle heat like that from a light bulb. But don't hold the paper too close. You can also use an iron on low heat, but don't use fire. Here's another fun way to do it: Write with milk (using a fine paintbrush) on thick cardstock or cardboard. You can rub graphite, ash, or powdered charcoal over it to reveal the words.[170]

Project
Watermark

You can create a watermark that is invisible until the paper is wet. Submerge a piece of paper in water and then press it flat against a hard surface such as a wall, mirror, or window. Then position a dry sheet of paper over it. Write on the dry sheet of paper with a pen or pencil. A ballpoint pen works best; if using a pencil, be sure it's not too sharp. Press firmly. Throw away the dry sheet, the one that shows what you wrote. You should be able to see the writing on the wet paper. But, when the paper dries, it will vanish—until you make it wet again.[171]

Word-Witch Practice
Pen, Pencil, and Ink

Here are some ideas and activities to try.

- The act of writing with a pencil and erasing can be a magical act in itself. Write the name of something you want to be rid of (a bad habit, for example) and visualize it vanishing as you erase it.

- Based on the materials it's made from, a pencil is a very "earthy" tool; consider using one for written spells involving the Earth Element (see chapter 20).

- Consider using colored pencils for your magical writing (see the Colorful Writing section in chapter 14).

---

170. Martin Gardner, *Codes, Ciphers, and Secret Writing* (New York: Dover Publications, Inc., 1972), Kindle.

171. Gardner, *Codes, Ciphers, and Secret Writing.*

- The act of writing the name of something you wish to banish and crossing it out can be a powerful word spell all on its own. Don't forget that the "simple" act of writing can be the spell.

- Consider writing out your favorite spells in your own handwriting; make a book of them, if you haven't already. Creating your own Book of Shadows this way gives it extra-personal energy. Make it pretty if you'd like. Try your hand (pun intended!) at calligraphy. Use stencils. Add symbols and images too.

- When using written magic in spells, try the technique of repetition— writing the same word or phrase over and over, like Bart Simpson writing on the chalkboard. While that act is intended as punishment, the goal is similar: if you write it down enough, you'll remember it. Magically speaking, you are writing your goal into existence.

CHAPTER 13

Paper

There's Nothing Plain about It

"By recording your dreams and goals on paper, *you* can set in motion the process of becoming the person you most want to be."
Mark Victor Hansen, *Future Diary*

Papyrus was the first paper, made from plants native to the land around the Nile. The ancient Egyptians used this plant for other things as well—they not only ate parts of the plant, but also used it for fashioning rope and making boats. The oldest known papyrus paper is at least 5,100 years old. Making the sheets of papyrus that could be written on was a laborious process; around the sixth century BCE, the Greeks began importing it before eventually creating their own, which they began to export.[172]

Since papyrus wasn't native to Europe (and it was expensive to import), other materials were used, including bark, tablets made of wood or wax, metal sheets, even plant leaves. Parchment was a later development, adopted from the East, using the stretched skin of animals such as calves, goats, sheep, and sometimes deer. These sheets were easily "stitched together to make books," which were more convenient to use than scrolls. Eventually, linen rags began to be turned into paper in the fifteenth century in Europe.[173]

---

172. Zender, *Writing and Civilization*, 184–85.

173. Davies, *Grimoires*.

The use of the word *paper* can be followed back through French and to the Classical Latin *papyrus*. "The Latin word already referred to paper in the conventional sense, but Latin had itself borrowed the term from Greek (*papyros*)," which was primarily used to refer to the papyrus plant before being applied to the writing material. However, the Greek word didn't originate with them, and it is believed they used words borrowed from Semitic.[174]

Paper as we know it today is made from a variety of plants, such as cotton, flax, and wood that are pulverized by a method of soaking, sometimes using heat, and then shredded and smashed into a pulp before drying. It has been made this way for more than two thousand years; of course, today the process has been automated and modernized. This type of papermaking is believed to have originated in China, and the technique quickly spread throughout Asia and the Middle East and eventually to Europe, replacing papyrus.[175]

Project
Handmade Paper

Paper varieties are as endless as pens and pencils, but there's something satisfying about making your own paper—and in knowing that you're participating in a skill that was used thousands of years ago. Your intent can make any craft a magical act, and papermaking is no exception. Handmade paper is a wonderful choice for creating written spells. You can infuse the paper with magical intent right from the start. As a bonus, you can also use the paper for other crafts, such as making cards or scrapbooking. However, sometimes this type of paper doesn't fold or roll very well, so keep that in mind if part of your spell involves those actions.

Making paper like this is a great way to recycle junk mail or old newspapers and magazines. Just about any type of paper can be used, but avoid the plastic window in some envelopes. Results will vary widely depending on the process

---

174. Zender, *Writing and Civilization*, 183.

175. Zender, *Writing and Civilization*, 185–86.

you use—the paper scraps you start with, how finely you mash the pulp, any additives you use, and so on. It's fun to experiment with various techniques and materials. It can be done indoors or out, on a small scale or large. The internet has made crafting easier than ever with endless video tutorials and instructions, but I'll go over the basics here.

Materials

- mold and deckle set (purchase or make your own)
- bits of scrap paper
- hot water
- large container with a lid
- something to mash the paper with—either a mortar and pestle or blender
- container large enough for the mold and deckle to fit inside—a dish pan often works well
- towels

You can buy a mold and deckle at a craft store or make your own. One easy way to start is by using old picture frames—that's what I did. Find two wooden frames that are the same size and remove the glass. On one of them, staple some window screen to the edges of the flattest side. (Make sure it's tight.) You will need to use some type of industrial-strength stapler. The other frame will be stacked on top of the one with the screen, keeping the paper mesh in place (more on that process later). The frame is the deckle; the piece with the screen attached is the mold. If you don't have the means to make or buy a mold and deckle, you can simply strain the pulp and spread it on a cookie sheet lined with newspaper or a thin cotton towel.

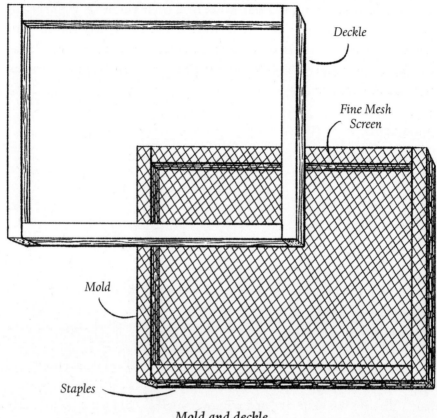

Mold and deckle

The main goal for this process is to create a paper pulp or "mash" that will be formed into a sheet and dried. There are many ways to create this pulp. You can cut or tear several sheets of paper into small pieces or use a paper shredder. The smaller the pieces, the less time it will take to create the pulp. How much you make in each batch is up to you.

After tearing or shredding, put your paper pieces into a jar or other container that has a lid. Pour several cups of hot water over the paper, cover it, and let it sit. You may want to stir it around with a wooden spoon to be sure all the paper is covered. You can let it sit overnight, but if you're using hot water and the paper pieces are very small, you may be able to begin the next step in a few hours.

Next, you will pulverize the wet paper pieces. You can use a blender, but be sure you don't use it for food again after this. Consider buying a used one for this purpose. You can also use a mortar and pestle or a sturdy bowl and wooden spoon or whisk. The goal here is to mash the wet paper into a paste-like consistency. Do this in small batches; just scoop out wet clumps of paper with your hands and mash. The finer you mash it, the smoother your finished paper will be.

Add water to a large bowl or other container (a plastic dishpan works well). Make sure it's large enough for your mold and deckle to fit inside. Fill it about three-quarters with water, and then add the paper pulp. At this stage, you can add extra decorative elements to the water—bits of herbs, flower petals, etc. Dip the mold and deckle (the deckle should be on top of the mold) into the water and swirl everything around so the bits of paper collect on the screen. Then gently lift the mold and deckle out of the water. Let the water drip off for a few moments, and then remove the deckle (frame) from the mold (frame with screen). Turn the mold over onto a cotton towel or other type of cloth to transfer the paper pulp. Press a sponge on the back of the screen—this serves the purpose of absorbing water. The more water you can remove from the pulp, the better. Next, lift the screen off the paper. Repeat this process to use all the pulp.

Drying time will vary—I typically use my basement for crafting, so it can take a few days for the paper to dry. It will dry faster in a warm, sunny place. You can even hang it. The paper should be stuck to the towel, so you can clip it to a hanger if you'd like. Or you can place it on a drying rack so air can flow easily around it. A baker's rack works well.

The final color will depend on what you use to make your paper. The first batch I made contained some newsprint, and the final sheets of paper, while still flecked with some color from other papers I used, had a gray overtone. However, the color did lighten as the paper dried, and it ended up being pale gray flecked with color and a few random bits of herbs that I added. It was actually quite pretty.

You may need to experiment with thickness. My first batch was somewhat uneven. In my first attempt, I didn't have the pulp ground very fine, and my mold and deckle (8" × 10" picture frames) didn't fit inside the pan I was using for water (silly me, I didn't test it first!). I had to smear the paper pulp over the screen, and the result was a very uneven sheet. However, it still worked. I still ended up with useful handmade paper. As with any craft, there's a learning curve when you're new. Practice will help. It's not a terribly messy craft, so have fun with it.

This paper will most likely not be as pliable as regular paper. If you try to roll it, it could fall apart. Again, it depends on the thickness and the fineness of your pulp. The very imperfect first piece I made was foldable but didn't roll well. The paper you end up with will most likely be somewhat soft, almost felt-like in texture. There are many variables since it all depends on the materials you start with and how finely you mash the pulp. Unless you're using it for art projects, don't worry too much about its appearance. If you're using it for magical purposes and simply need to write on it, that's all that really matters.

Here's a sample chant you can use to infuse your paper with energy:

New purpose to serve,
new goals to fulfill;
let this paper be fused
with intent as I will.

Tips

- As you shred or tear the paper, visualize the paper being cleared of all previous energy.
- Make each part of the process an aspect of ritual. For example, place the soaking paper in moonlight or sunlight—you can even add a few drops of essential oil (be sure to use a carrier oil) or herbs to the water.
- You can chant or sing throughout the process or recite other things—prayers, affirmations, etc. Play music or burn incense during the process if you wish. Visualize your magical intent during every part of the process. The finished product will be infused with your energy.
- Make seed paper by adding flower or herb seeds to your paper, so when it's buried, plants will grow—these also make great gifts!
- You can state a specific goal while creating your paper or let it remain open, simply charging the new paper for general magical use.

Stamping and Scrapbooking

No discussion of magical writing and paper would be complete without mentioning the popularity of stamping and scrapbooking—hobbies that run the spectrum between very simple rubber stamps, ink, and paper to equipment that creates fancy patterns and cutouts, decorative ribbons, punches, embossing, and so much more. I love creating handmade cards and using many of these techniques.

I once made some gift bags for friends that each contained a little spell scroll. I used plain paper but made it look "antique" with special inks and then tore the edges. I wrote the spell on the paper and rolled it, then tied it with a ribbon. Projects like this are fun and make lovely gifts.

You can purchase stamps that contain words and phrases or create your own with stamps that are letters of the alphabet. This process can be just as magical as writing, as long as you create with intent.

Curse Tablets

Making your own curse tablet is easy using materials like paper or a sheet of wax (see chapter 14), but if you want a metallic look and feel, use aluminum foil. The key is to use a thin sheet so you can roll it and pierce it with a nail. I've even done it with paper or leaves and punctured them with a thorny rose stem.

A word about cursing: If you're actually going to curse someone, use caution. If you've been ill-treated, consider a plea for justice or the return of stolen property, the righting of a wrong done against you. There are other alternatives too, such as banishing—removing the influence from your life or preventing it from causing harm. These are a bit less severe than cursing. Of course, a "curse tablet" doesn't actually have to contain a "curse." By their very nature, these spells are intended as a form of seeking justice—inflicting harm on someone need not be part of the spell.

You can deposit the amulet into a body of water as the ancients did, but that may not be the most environmentally friendly method, depending on the material you use. A better option would be to bury it. If you really want to destroy it, use paper and burn it, and then either bury the ashes, release them on the wind, or flush them down the toilet. Personally, I save the flushing method only for things I really want to banish—there's something satisfying about imagining the object of banishment ending up with the sewage.

See chapter 20 (The Elements) for a variety of ways to get rid of an amulet. One technique is to "freeze someone out" by soaking a paper textual amulet in water and then putting it in the freezer.

Project
DIY Curse Tablet

Here's a simple process to make your own personalized curse tablet.

Materials

- One sheet of paper or aluminum foil (even a fresh leaf would work for this purpose or a pliable sheet of wax)—size is your choice.
- Nail or toothpick to pierce the paper or other material. (If you have a large piece of paper or foil, you may need several items to fasten it together. Consider using plant thorns for this purpose if they are strong enough to pierce the material you're using.)
- Writing implement—the surface you choose will determine what you write with.

Create sacred space and include other spell materials as desired. To create the curse tablet, write your word or phrase on the paper (or other material). You can also add symbols if you wish. Remember to visualize your goal and state your intent out loud, if you wish. You can simply recite what you're writing or compose an accompanying chant. When you're ready, roll the paper or foil into a tube (or fold it) and pierce it with the nails or toothpicks. An alternate method is to roll it first and then flatten it. Dispose of the tablet as desired—burying, burning, freezing, etc. If you choose burning and are left with the nails, bury them. For the freezing option, you decide how long to keep the item in the freezer before disposing of it.

Curse Tablet Example

Word-Witch Practice

Paper

Try these activities to enhance your magical work with paper.

- Consider repurposing all kinds of things to write on, such as cardboard from food packages, junk mail envelopes, paper bags, craft bags, calendars, etc. Parchment paper used for baking is also a good choice, as is butcher paper, tissue paper, etc. Those cardboard tubes inside paper towel and bath tissue rolls can be written on—a great way to utilize spiral or circular symbolism.

- Try paper-mache or decoupage to create interesting surfaces to write on, or to add special words and phrases to an object. You can glue paper to almost any surface—flowerpots, lamps, furniture, etc. I once tore apart old paperback novels and used the sheets to decoupage an entire bookcase.

- Experiment with folding techniques. To banish, fold the paper away from you; to draw something to you, fold the paper toward yourself. If you're adept at origami, you can use that in magic—write on paper before you fold it. Consider the shape of the fold and number of times to fold it (see chapter 17). You can also roll paper, crumple it, etc. Make a paper fortune teller—kids aren't the only ones who enjoy them!

- Wrap a written spell around a crystal or other stone, or write on paper and bury it.

- There's a craft trend of making altered books—taking existing books and not only re-covering them but pasting over the existing pages and decorating them. You can use decoupage and other techniques; use this idea to create a Book of Shadows.

- The ancient Maya made offerings of blood dripped onto ritual paper. The paper was burned, and the smoke could be inhaled to induce visions.[176] While inhaling this smoke may not be the best idea considering chemicals in the paper, you could try this technique for other purposes. For example, put a drop of your own blood on paper and burn or bury the paper as part of a ritual. You could do this with spit as well.

- If you want to flush a written spell, consider writing it on toilet tissue.

- Did you know there are edible papers and inks? Bakeries have been creating edible photos for cakes for a long time now, but you can do it at home. You can buy cartridges of edible ink for your printer and edible paper. You can also buy little kits of edible paper that come with a pen filled with edible ink to write with. These are often marketed to kids but can definitely be used for magical purposes. With edible paper and edible ink, you can create a spell you can literally (and safely) consume (more on food in chapter 15). If you want to try your hand at making

---

176. *A History of Magic, Witchcraft and the Occult*, 59.

your own edible paper, there are tutorials online. They're typically made from rice flour or potato starch.

- You can purchase flash paper—special treated paper that literally goes up in flames in a "flash" when ignited.

CHAPTER 14

Beyond Paper

Other Surfaces and Substances

"Words have power. And they can't be taken back."
Alice Hoffman, *Magic Lessons*

Moving beyond paper for magical writing is worth the effort. I encourage you to experiment with the variety of items discussed in this chapter and try some of the projects. Even if some of this is familiar territory, there are bound to be a few surprises or new things to try.

Wood and Leaves

Wood crafters know that there are specific types of wood that are more suitable than others for certain purposes. Some woods are hard, others are soft; some make excellent furniture, others don't. In folklore, we have come to ascribe various meanings to plants and trees based on their characteristics. We can apply that same knowledge here. Choose a type of wood or leaf that corresponds to your particular spell. Writing on wood and leaves is certainly a very "earthy" type of magic; however, you can use these methods for any type of spell.

While fresh leaves are probably easy to find, you may be wondering how to obtain pieces of wood (assuming you're not an experienced woodworker). The easiest way is to purchase them at craft stores. You could also walk in the woods and pick up pieces of fallen logs or tree bark. (Be sure you have permission if it's not your property).

When you attempt to write on a leaf or piece of wood, don't worry about how it looks—what matters most is the act of doing it and the action you take.

Project

Oak Leaf Money Spell

This simple spell is intended for use with an oak leaf, but can easily be adapted.

Materials

- oak leaf—fresh, if possible
- something to write with

Any type of oak leaf will do. If you don't have access to an oak leaf, you can use any type of leaf that is associated with prosperity. Using a pen or marker, write the words "money" on one side and "abundance" on the other. Of course, as you do this, you should visualize your specific need. You can write an accompanying chant or affirmation if you wish. Next, there are a couple options for what to do with the leaf. You can try carrying it with you until it's dry (if using a fresh leaf). Fresh leaves are usually easy to roll or fold, making this a good option for placement in a wallet or purse, or in a drawstring bag with other materials such as herbs or crystals of your choice. Another option is to keep the leaf on your altar until the spell manifests or you decide to discard the leaf. Burying is a good option since the act of burying something in the earth is typically associated with growth and nurturing.

Word-Witch Practice
Wood and Leaves

Try these ideas for working with wood and leaves.

- Practice writing on fresh leaves to see which pen works best for your situation. I've had good luck with ballpoint pens, fountain pens, and felt-tip markers. You can also try writing on dried leaves if they're sturdy enough.

- Smooth planks of wood are the easiest to write on with a pen or pencil, but don't forget about sticks and tree bark. For all these types of wood, felt-tip markers are a good option—especially the metallic colors like silver and gold. You can also use acrylic paint or purchase a paint pen (see chapter 12 for more ideas).

- For magic that involves emotions, cleansing, or intellectual pursuits (Elements of Air or Water), write your key word or phrase on a leaf or piece of wood and either float it on a body of water (ideally down a stream) or let it blow away on the wind. If you're using a dry leaf, a wind release works great if you crumble the leaf into pieces. This is especially useful if you're trying to dispel something.

- For magic that involves growth or fertility or, alternately, a gentle banishing (Element of Earth), write your words on a leaf or piece of wood and bury it.

- If your purpose is one that concerns transformation or passion, or a more forceful type of destructive banishment (Element of Fire), after writing on the leaf or wood, burn it. For this type of work, you may want to toss the leaf into a fire rather than trying to light it, or use a dried leaf. (Burning fresh leaves is not as easy as it seems; it can be difficult for them to catch fire and burn completely.) You can release the ashes on the wind, bury them, or deposit them into water. See chapter 20 for more ideas—the method you choose depends on the purpose of your spell.

- Carving a word or phrase into a piece of wood with a knife is another method to try, but use caution and don't cut yourself! If you have the skill, you can carve the wood into a shape or burn words and images into the wood. Use your creativity!

Correspondences for Different Types of Wood and Leaves

Here are some correspondences to guide your choice of plant materials.

Oak: sun, projective, Fire; protection, fertility, luck, health, money, healing

Hickory: sun, projective, Fire: endurance, strength, legal matters

Juniper: sun, projective, Fire; protection, love, anti-theft, exorcism, health

Walnut: sun, projective, Fire; health, mental powers, infertility, wishes

Persimmon: receptive, Venus, Water; healing, luck

Maple: projective, Jupiter, Air; love, money, longevity

Birch: receptive, Venus, Water; protection, exorcism, purification

Pine: projective, Mars, Air; healing, fertility, protection, money, exorcism

Elder: receptive, Venus, Water; protection, healing, prosperity, sleep, exorcism

Rowan: projective, sun, Fire; healing, psychic abilities, protection, success, magical power

Clay

Craft clay is fun to work with; I've used it for dozens of projects over the years. One of the easiest ways to write on clay is to make a "sheet" or "tablet" on which you can engrave or carve words and symbols. Using air-dry clay is convenient since you don't need to bake it (of course, that's an option if you choose). You can purchase craft clay at hobby shops and online. I use the Activa brand, but there are others.

Project
Clay Banishing Tablet

In ancient Egypt, names of people to be cursed were written on pots that were ritually smashed, burned, and buried.[177] This type of magical action can be very effective for banishing.

Materials

- rolling pin
- craft clay
- toothpick or other writing implement

Using a rolling pin, smooth out a handful of clay to the desired thickness (you may want to dedicate a rolling pin specifically for this purpose). Protect the surface of your work area with waxed paper for easier cleanup, or work on a glass surface protector. You can also work on a plate, and if you just want to work the clay with your hands instead of rolling it out, that's fine too. There's really no wrong way to do this. You can make an oval, circle, square, or any other shape you desire. Don't make it too thin; it will shrink as it dries and could crumble.

While it's still soft, add your desired writing—symbols, words, etc. You can use a toothpick or other sharp object. Then let the clay dry. It can take a couple days, depending on the humidity level in your workspace. Also, while it's still soft, you can roll it if you wish, hiding your message inside. When the piece is completely dry, you're ready to break it, dispose of it, or take whatever action is next in your ritual.

---

177. *A History of Magic, Witchcraft and the Occult*, 24.

Project
Spell Stone

I have a decorative bowl in my entryway that contains potpourri, dried flowers, crystals, pine cones, and other things. On top of the pile is a stone that features the words "Blessed Be." You can easily make one of these by shaping a lump of craft clay and carving words into it. If you can find a rubber stamp that contains your desired message, press that into the clay instead. After the piece dries, you can paint it if you wish. Sealing the piece with Mod Podge is also a good idea. This is also an easy way to utilize the One-Word Spell (see chapter 11). These can be displayed or kept hidden, depending on your goal. They look nice in decorative bowls or even in the garden.

Word-Witch Practice
Clay

Try these ideas for working with clay.

- You can create your own piece that resembles an ancient stone tablet from Mesopotamia with your own secret symbols and letters, use an existing magical alphabet, or simply write in your own language.
- You can press herbs or stones into the clay before drying it.

Wax

Carving words on candles is a common aspect of candle magic. But there are other ways to add words to wax. The easiest way is to purchase beeswax sheets. You can even find kits for making candles that come with wax sheets and wicks. Simply use a toothpick or other sharp object to carve your word or words into the wax (the smooth side is easiest—the inside of the candle), then roll it according to the package directions and make your candle.

If you're comfortable working with wax, you can make a "sheet" of wax to write on. One reason creating with wax that you melt yourself is special is that you can make the melting process part of the spell. You can visualize and chant during the entire process, adding more personal energy to the act. This can be done by purchasing blocks of wax from a craft store or by saving wax from spent candles and reusing it.[178]

Project
Wax Sheet

Here's an easy method to make a wax sheet.

Materials

- chunks of wax—amount varies
- double boiler
- cookie sheet
- waxed paper
- toothpick or other object to "write" with
- candle or candy thermometer

If you've never worked with wax, be sure you follow the directions carefully and always use a thermometer to monitor the temperature. Basically, the double-boiler method is easiest for melting wax. If you don't have one, you can use a carafe or can inserted into a pot of boiling water instead. The double-boiler method is basically the act of melting the wax in a container that is placed inside a pot of water. You heat the water, and the heat generated by the hot water melts the wax. Be sure the wax doesn't get above 300°F. An ideal temperature for pouring is between 160° and 175°F.

Line a cookie sheet with waxed paper and pour the hot wax onto it. When the wax is soft and pliable but not yet hard, you can carve into it with a toothpick.

---

178. My book *Magical Candle Crafting* explores in detail the process of making candles for magical use.

Even after the wax is dry, you can still engrave it, but it's easier to work with if it's not completely hardened. What you do next is up to you. One option is to roll the wax while it's still pliable, after you write on it, and let it dry in that shape, just like you would a beeswax sheet. After it's dry, you can break it, dispose of it, etc.

Glass

You can write with markers or paint on glass and mirrors very easily. Another fun way to mark on glass is etching. Most craft stores carry etching cream, and you can even buy kits that come with brushes and stencils to create designs and words. Armour Etch is the brand I'm most familiar with, but there are others on the market. Liquid chalk markers and pens are a perfect way to write on windows and other types of glass. The best part about this option is that it can be washed off.

Word-Witch Practice
Glass

Here are some ways to enhance your glass magic.

- You can etch words onto mirrors to use as an amulet or talisman.
- Etch words onto glass bottles used for storing herbs and supplies, or create a protection bottle.
- When I was a kid, I liked to write in glue on old mirrors and then sprinkle glitter on the glue. You can use glitter glue, markers, or paint for this. (Use glitter sparingly; it's hazardous to the environment.)
- Write a positive affirmation or key word(s) around the edges of the mirror—words you'll see each time you look at your reflection. You can use a large bathroom mirror or a handheld compact. You could write the word *confidence* or *I am beautiful* or any other positive statement. Lipstick also writes well on mirrors.

- Write on steam-covered mirrors in the bathroom. When we first moved in together, my husband and I used to leave messages like this for each other.
- A key word can be written on a glass candleholder with an eye- or lip-liner pencil. You can also write a longer statement, such as an affirmation or spell.

Bones

Some people avoid working with bones in magic because they think it's bizarre or it makes them uncomfortable. This is understandable. Bones represent something that we all must face—our own mortality. Even just holding the bone of an animal can be a vivid reminder of this reality. But that's one of the reasons I believe it's important to try working with bones at least once. If you don't have access to bones, check with local butcher shops or places that process meat.

I used to feel somewhat uneasy when I found bones in the woods. I wondered, should I bury them? Keep them? But now I'm thrilled to find them, and I typically collect them (while offering thanks), unless I find the full body of an animal—then I leave it alone. Any time I find bones, I'm filled with an overwhelming sense of respect for the creature and its life. Using bones in this way can be a powerful part of your magical practice. You can simply use them on your altar to symbolize the cycle of life or make them part of a ritual, spell, or affirmation.

I've found that pencils and felt-tip markers are the best choice for writing on bone. I've tried both art pencils and a variety of colored pencils, all with success. You can also use acrylic paint, especially if you find a bone that hasn't aged well and is discolored and doesn't look nice even after you clean it. You can write with paint or paint the entire bone before writing on it with a different color of paint, pencil, or marker. In addition, you can paint over previous writing and start fresh using the same bone for a new purpose.

Project
DIY Oracle Bone

In ancient China, there was a divination practice of consulting the oracle bones. A question would be written on a piece of bone (often a cow shoulder or turtle shell), then the diviner would apply a heated poker, touching the bone, causing cracks to form. The cracks would then be interpreted, and the "answer" (whatever the diviner believed it to be) would then be written on the bone as well. Later the outcome would also be recorded. The bone would be threaded on a cord or stick with other oracle bones as an archive.[179]

You can try this yourself if you have access to a cow bone, for example, or one from a deer. If you ever come across the bones of an armadillo, the plate-like pieces are good to use for this purpose as well; turtle shells are also a good option. Do not take the life of any creature for such a purpose—use materials that you find or can obtain from others who have found them, or ones that have been respectfully used as food.

Use a pencil or marker to write your question on the bone. To apply heat, you could use a tool such as a soldering iron or place the bone near or among the hot coals of a fire. Once cracks have appeared, carefully remove the bone from the heat source and let it rest for a few minutes. Interpret the cracks: this requires your own personal insight. If you wish, you can then write down your interpretation (either on the bone or elsewhere, such as in a journal). Remain aware over time for the outcome. Record that as well (again, either on the bone or in a journal).

Writing with Water

One day I was sitting on a large, flat rock near the creek in our woods. I dipped my finger in the water to write words and draw symbols on the stone and watched as they dried and faded away. That moment was the inspiration for this chapter.

---

179. Robinson, The Story of Writing, 183.; John R. Hale, *Exploring the Roots of Religion*, part 2 (Chantilly, VA: The Teaching Company, 2009), 43.

Just like writing in sand and letting the wind blow your words away, you can "write" with water. There are several approaches you can take. One way to do this is to visualize that you're charging the stone (or other surface) as you write on it with water. Imagine the stone holds and keeps the power in it. If it's a small stone, you can carry it with you. On the other hand, you can write a message that vanishes to represent something you wish to diminish or be rid of. Another aspect of this technique is the actual act of "writing" in the body of water with your finger (or a small paintbrush, stick, or other item).

Just as a white candle serves all purposes, you can get by with simple tap water for your water writing magic. However, using a special type of water (or other liquid) is one way to enhance your experience. Of course, always use only clean water and use caution if you plan to drink it. If you have well water at your home rather than water provided by a city or county, then you're a step closer to its source. There are fewer channels the water has to go through, and it's closer to its original state. When I use tap water, I know it's coming from a well on my property; however, sometimes I go straight to the well pump to draw it—it just feels closer to nature. And if I really want to feel close to nature, I collect water from our creek—although I won't drink that water, just to be safe, because there could be runoff in it from the nearby farms. Water you've collected requires more energy and effort than turning on the tap, so it gives your spell more power. Be mindful where you collect, and be sure you have permission and that the water is safe to use.

The qualities of different types of water also deserve some consideration. For a spell that requires action, choose water from a moving source if possible—for example, a running stream or rainwater. For a more calming effect, choose still water (but not stagnant), such as from a pond or lake. Melted ice or snow is an excellent choice for a spell that involves transformation. While you could argue that all water transforms, having actual melted snow or ice means this is water that was recently transformed.

While I have rocks in mind for this type of magic, you can use other surfaces as well, such as wood or bone. I like to use rock because you can see what you've written while it's still wet and then watch it dry. Experiment with different types of rock, brick, landscaping stones, and other objects to see what works best for your situation.

Project
Water Writing Spell for Health

Here's an easy spell that uses water and stone.

Materials

- water of your choice
- small, clean paintbrush
- stone or other object large enough to write on

First, decide if you want to write on a small stone (or other object) that you can carry with you or on a large rock that will remain in place. Collect your desired water. You will either write with the small paintbrush or you can use your finger. You can write just one word (see One-Word Spell, chapter 11) or a longer statement. You could write *good health* or *healing* or something more specific. Alternately, you can write the name of an illness or condition and visualize it vanishing as the words fade. Accompany your spell with the appropriate visualization and recite additional words as desired.

Here are some sample statements:

Water, let this word I write
conjure and fulfill my need;
water, as I form [this word or these words]
let this magic spell succeed.

or

This word I write
will grant my will;
this word I write
my needs fulfill.

Repeat the spell as desired.

Word-Witch Practice
Water Writing

This is another easy spell for using water for writing. Before creating your elixir, though, be sure the stone you're using is safe to submerge in water.

- Make a crystal elixir and use this water to write with.
- Essential oils can be used to write just like using them to anoint objects. You can also do this on your skin (see the section Words on the Body in chapter 15). Use a small brush. Be sure to follow the safety guidelines for the oils—some can cause irritation. Use a carrier oil such as jojoba or avocado oil.
- Obtain water from a local source such as a spring, lake, stream, pond, ocean, or well—just be sure you have permission.
- Using melted ice or snow, rain, or dewdrops is a wonderful way to engage with nature while you're collecting. You can incorporate the traits of the particular season into your spell or ritual. You can even make the act of gathering the water part of your ritual.
- Charge water in sunlight or moonlight before using it, depending on the characteristics of your work.
- Add herbs to the water, essential oils, or both. If using essential oils, be sure to use a carrier oil.
- Using salt water is a classic method of cleansing, but you can also write with it. Just be sure that the salt won't damage the surface you're using.
- Don't forget about working with steam—it's water vapor.

Colorful Writing

The use of certain colors for specific purposes in magic is well established. But beyond the choice of color for your candles, crystals, clothes, jewelry, and other items, don't forget about adding color to what you write. Color can enhance the meaning and mood of your expression in myriad ways.

It may seem obvious, but color is an easy way to utilize the One-Word Spell (chapter 11). Consider which color(s) resonate(s) with your key word; for example, red or pink for love, orange or gold for success, and so on. Next, choose the medium that best fits your goal. What do you want to write with? Chalk, crayon, pencil, ink, or paint? Choose an appropriate surface (don't forget that you can also use colored paper). Conjure your inner artist and focus on your goal as you create. For your convenience, there's a list of color correspondences at the end of this chapter.

Chalk

Chalk is actually a naturally occurring rock, mainly containing calcite. Depending on where you live, you may have found these soft pieces of rock that easily make marks on other surfaces. Chalk is famously known as the lovely White Cliffs of Dover in England. A type of limestone, chalk is mostly made of fragments of shells or plankton, and the majority of it formed during the Cretaceous period, between 66 and 145 million years ago. In fact, since these deposits are so common, the name Cretaceous comes from them—Latin *creta*: "chalk."[180] This is also the origin of the word *crayon*. Tailors once used it to mark on fabric, although today products made from talc are more common. And in sports, chalk has been used to mark lines on playing fields, but again, other chemicals have replaced the use of chalk. Chalk is commonly used in construction materials as an additive. It can also be manufactured to create the chalk used to write on blackboards as well as colored chalk. These types are typically made from gypsum.[181]

Have you ever done chalk art on a sidewalk? It's fun and it washes away. Chalk can be an excellent choice if your spell involves using a word that's impermanent—for example, if the spell is for a banishing and you want water to wash away the word. If your spell utilizes the Earth Element, then chalk is a good choice to write with. Because of its link to sea life, it can also relate to the Water Element. Chalk is an excellent choice for writing on concrete or stone.

---

180. Hobart M. King, "Chalk," Geology.com, accessed April 12, 2024, https://geology.com/rocks/chalk.shtml.

181. King, "Chalk."

Crayons

We may think of crayons as a modern invention, things kids use for coloring, but the technique of making crayons is thousands of years old. Crayons as we know them today are believed to have been invented in Europe and were first made from a mix of charcoal and oil. Eventually other pigments replaced the charcoal, and wax was used instead of oil. Pastels are another form of art medium, also made from pigments and a substance that binds the product. The type of binding agent creates the difference between a wax crayon and a pastel. Most crayons today are made from paraffin wax. Crayons, pastels, and colored pencils are all good choices if you want to employ the use of various colors and make your spell extra creative.

I remember using sheets of black "waxy" paper when I was a kid, which could be scraped to reveal colors beneath the black surface. I remember making these by using crayons to color paper and then using a black crayon to cover the colors and then scraping the black off to reveal the color underneath. The same method works for concealing a written spell. Write with a pencil and then obliterate it using crayons. You can scrape away the waxy crayon color to reveal the word or phrase.

Paint

There's a type of paint for just about everything you can imagine—from paper and canvas to wood and stone, metal and glass, ceramics, and more. You can spray it, brush it—there are even paint markers you can hold like a pen. Simple acrylic paints are good for many purposes and are inexpensive and widely available. The same goes for watercolor paints. These are great if you're a beginner since they're nontoxic, easy to clean up, and wash off most surfaces—like your hands!

Word-Witch Practice
Color

Try these ideas for working with color.

- Use acrylic paint on glass and mirrors, stone, clay, shells, bones, and wood.
- Glitter glue is fun and pretty, but glitter is hazardous to the environment. Use it sparingly.
- You can buy a pack of paintbrushes in various sizes and experiment with the results.
- And don't forget about liquid chalk markers used to write on window glass (See the Glass section of chapter 14)—these can sometimes be used on other surfaces, such as plastic.
- Another way to utilize color in your word magic is to consider the color of leaves and even flower petals that you can write on. Think of autumn leaves in red, orange, and yellow or the leaves of some plants that are more than just green—some are even pink or purple.
- You can buy pieces of colored glass at craft stores (I use these often since I'm a stained-glass artist). You can paint or write on these; some places even sell small scrap pieces so you don't have to buy a full sheet.
- Paint words on the wall of a room and then paint over them. You'll know they're there, even if no one can see them.
- Write the names of the Elements on quarter candleholders (in their appropriate colors). This is a great way to add color if you only have clear candleholders and white candles.

Basic Color Correspondences

Here are the traditional correspondences for working with color.

White: neutral, all-purpose, full moon energy, protection, meditation, initiation

Black: banishment, breaking bad habits, reversal spells

Red: protection, passion, energy, courage, strength, sexuality, will

Pink: romance, love, friendship, harmony, emotions

Orange: success, commerce, motivation, courage, legal problems

Yellow: mental skills, communication, self-confidence, charm, travel, health, success, power

Green: money, fertility, growth, abundance, health and healing

Dark blue: dream magic, transformation, instinct, psychic awareness, protection from the evil eye

Light blue: beginnings, endurance, awareness, joy

Pale violet: inspiration, divination

Dark purple: authority, leadership, mastery, spirituality, wisdom, psychic awareness, curse-breaking

Gray: neutrality, mystery, dimness, concealment, secrets

Brown: home, domestic issues, justice, grounding, animals, and nature

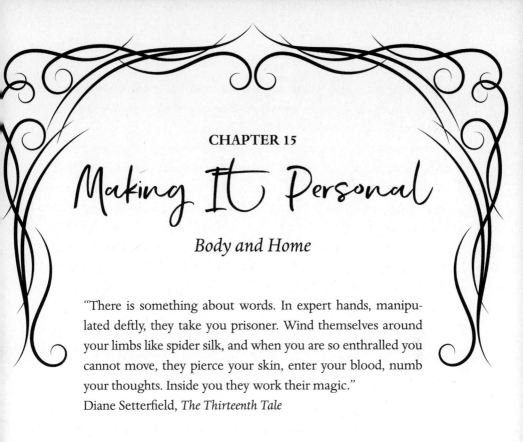

CHAPTER 15

Making It Personal

Body and Home

"There is something about words. In expert hands, manipulated deftly, they take you prisoner. Wind themselves around your limbs like spider silk, and when you are so enthralled you cannot move, they pierce your skin, enter your blood, numb your thoughts. Inside you they work their magic."
Diane Setterfield, *The Thirteenth Tale*

This chapter explores a variety of ways to use written word magic around the home and on the body. This includes food and other personal adornments and decorations.

Words on the Body

Writing on the skin is an ancient technique that has never seemed to wane in its modern popularity. Tattoos are one of the most popular ways to use the power of words (and images) on the body, and it's a tradition that goes back thousands of years and is present in cultures all over the world. We tattoo names on our bodies in remembrance or to show our love and devotion; tattoos of words and symbols inspire us and represent things that are meaningful to us.

The oldest recorded tattoo is 5,200 years old! Early tattoos were made using a needle-style instrument, often created from sharpened animal bones, and the pigments were often charcoal or other plant materials and dyes. Basically, the process hasn't changed much—the skin is pierced and pigment "injected."[182]

Luckily, though, you don't need to commit to a permanent tattoo if you don't want to; there are many methods to create temporary tattoos, including henna and special body paints. You can also just use makeup products like eyeliner or lip liner to write or draw on your skin. Just remember to use caution and avoid using ink or markers on your skin. Use only products intended to be used on the body.

When using a temporary tattoo for magic, when the word(s) wears off, the spell is complete, or you can deliberately wash it off as part of the spell, depending on your goal. For magic purposes, the placement on the body should be considered—particular locations have different correspondences.

It was once believed that illness was due to an imbalance in the body's four humors (phlegm, blood, and yellow and black bile), a theory developed by Hippocrates around 400 BCE. Medieval medicine often involved astrology, and specific signs of the zodiac were believed to influence various parts of the body. Magic has long been employed as a method of healing, and much early "medicine" was built around not only using plant materials but amulets, talismans, and other types of spells. Here are some of the correspondences for parts of the body and their various associations.

Astrological

Aries: head and face

Taurus: throat and neck

Gemini: shoulders, arms, and hands

Cancer: chest and stomach

Leo: heart and spine

Virgo: intestines and stomach

Libra: kidneys and back

Scorpio: genitals

---

182. Cate Lineberry, "The Worldwide History of Tattoos," *Smithsonian Magazine,* updated by Sonja Anderson, updated October 18, 2023, https://www.smithsonianmag.com/history/tattoos-worldwide-history-144038580/.

Sagittarius: liver, hips, and thighs

Capricorn: knees and shins

Aquarius: ankles

Pisces: feet

General Considerations

- The right side of the body has more masculine energy; the left, feminine.
- The right side of the body represents the past; the left, the future.
- Also consider your receptive and projective hands—the one you write with is typically projective and the other is receptive, but some people consider the left receptive and right projective no matter which one you write with.
- The thighs are places of strength and personal power.
- The feet and ankles are areas of support or grounding.
- The arm is a good place to display goals or dreams.
- The hips represent energy and motion.
- The abdomen is a place of nurturing.
- The chest is a place of emotions.
- The forehead is associated with the third eye.
- Also consider the chakras for locations of tattoos.

Fingers and Planetary Associations Based on Palmistry

- Index finger, pointer finger, Jupiter: leadership and confidence
- Middle finger, Saturn: logic and material life
- Ring finger, Apollo/Sun: fortune and expansion; motivation
- Little finger, Mercury: intellect, communication, humanitarian pursuits
- Thumb, Venus: often associated with logic and determination

Other Adornments

Self-expression is an integral part of who we are—the way we dress, wear our hair, our choice of jewelry, and more. All of these things are avenues for magical expression, if you wish. Consider all the possibilities with makeup, nail polish, and other accessories. Charm bracelets that feature words are an easy way to utilize wearable magic language. Use nail polish to write a letter on each nail to spell a word or phrase. You can keep it visible or, after it's dry, paint over it to hide it. You can use both hands, or consider writing something you want on your receptive hand and something you want to project on your dominant hand. If you have a locket that opens or a poison ring, you can write on a small piece of paper and carry it with you that way. Pieces of paper or other small amulets and talismans can also be tucked into pockets or undergarments, shoes and socks, handbags, etc.

Word-Witch Practice
Words on the Body

Try these ideas for ways to wear magic words.

- Use essential oils or perfume; for example, write the word *love* on the inner arm of your receptive hand using a paintbrush. Remember to use a carrier oil when working with essential oils on the skin.
- Writing on the body can be a group ritual—writing on each other's arms or backs, for example.
- Write a word on the appropriate finger, or fashion a slip of paper that contains words into a ring to wear. Use a ring as an amulet on a specific finger.

Word Magic in the Home

There's a trend in modern home decor of displaying words as art—"Live, Laugh, Love," for example, or signs that say, "Follow Your Dreams" or "Bless This Home." In some ways, this is a form of magic. We use these phrases as reminders and to essentially evoke those qualities in our lives. But there are other ways to do this if that's not your style. You can be more subtle and more creative. You can basically put words anywhere—visible or hidden. Here are some ideas to get you started.

You can literally write a spell and put it anywhere—write *prophetic dreams* or *restful sleep* on a small piece of paper and tuck it inside your pillowcase. To get even more creative, use the appropriate colored ink, for example, and maybe even use handmade paper or write on the leaf of a plant associated with your goal.

When we were painting our house before selling it, my husband and I had fun writing messages to each other in the paint before painting over it. You could do that for a spell in a new residence. Paint a message—a protection spell, for example—then paint over it, knowing it's technically still there, even though you can't see it.

Food

Food magic can be very simple or extremely complex—there's something for everyone! I remember when I was a kid, my mom would write my name with pancake batter or create shapes like hearts. As a form of kitchen witchery, you can obviously use magic while you're cooking, but the techniques listed here mainly involve writing on food so you can eat it (if necessary).

Word-Witch Practice
Food

Try these ideas for using food with word magic.

- As mentioned in the section on paper, an easy way to create magic you can literally consume is to buy edible paper and inks.
- You can use a toothpick to carve a word on a slice of cheese, then simply eat it. You can also fold the cheese or put it on a sandwich if you'd like to hide the word.
- Some of the easiest things to write on include cheese, crackers, cake, and cookies, but don't forget about bread, butter, and fruits.
- You can "write" or "etch" on foods such as potato, apple, etc.—the peel or the flesh—and even eat it, depending on what you write with.

- This may be an obvious one, but you can write with glaze or gel frosting on cakes and cookies. There are even edible "markers" for writing on cookies.
- While stirring something, you can "write" in the batter or liquid.
- If you want to use the method of letting ink dissolve into liquid so you can drink it, be sure to use edible ink and paper.
- Trace words into cornmeal, sugar, flour, or other substances before using in cooking or allowing the wind to disperse the material.

Food Correspondences

This is not a complete list, of course, just some of the foods easiest to write on or carve.

Potato: receptive, moon, Earth—healing, image magic

Apple: receptive, Venus, Water—love, healing, garden magic, immortality

Avocado: receptive, Venus, Water—love, lust, beauty

Bay: projective, sun, Fire—protection, healing, strength, purification, psychic powers

Beet: receptive, Saturn, Earth—love

Carrot: projective, Mars, Fire—fertility, lust

Radish: projective, Mars, Fire—protection, lust

Turnip: receptive, Moon, Earth—protection, ending relationships

Corn (use the husks): receptive, Venus, Earth—protection, luck, divination

Cabbage: receptive, Moon, Water—luck

Lettuce: receptive, Moon, Water—chastity, protection, love, divination, sleep

Cucumber: receptive, Moon, Water—chastity, healing, fertility

Pumpkin: receptive, Moon, Earth—sexual arousal, prosperity

Lemon: receptive, Moon, Water—purification and cleansing, love, friendship, health

Leek: projective, Mars, Fire—protection, love, exorcism

Lime: projective, Sun, Fire—protection, love, healing, purification

The Home: Inside and Out

There's no way to cover all the possibilities of using word magic in the home. Basically, anywhere you can write or attach a written spell or affirmation presents an opportunity for magic. Begin by considering your goal and which location best suits your purpose. Does your goal include a group of people? If so, target rooms where people gather to eat and talk, such as the kitchen, living room, or dining room. Or is your goal personal—just for the people who live in the home? What about guests or unwanted visitors? Consider thresholds—windows and doors—for protection spells, as well as outdoor spaces, property lines, and fences. Of course, whether or not you want your spell to be hidden or seen is also a deciding factor. Here are some projects to try.

Project
Garden Stone

You may already have statues or other objects with words on them in your garden or on your patio or deck, but if not, you can easily make your own. You can paint a phrase on the bottom of an item, such as a flowerpot, or make something artistic and visible, such as a garden stone. The easiest way to create a garden stone is to start with a rock that you've found—the smoother the better. Be sure the stone has been thoroughly washed. Using paint or a marker, write a key word or phrase on the stone. An alternate method is to paint the entire rock first, then write your word or words on it. If desired, seal the stone with Mod Podge to protect the paint from rain (depending on the type of paint you used). You can use words like *grow* or *peace* and add symbols too. Another method to create a garden stone involves using craft clay (see the Clay section of chapter 14). You can press words from rubber stamps into the clay, let it dry, then paint it.

Project
Witch Bottle

Here's an example of a witch bottle that combines several of the techniques we've discussed so far. Witch bottles can be made to serve just about any purpose and include everything from pretty glass bottles to regular jars or other containers. They can be displayed as decorative items or hidden in your home. Traditionally, these types of bottles include an assortment of herbs and salt, but also nails, broken glass, and, in some cases, bodily fluids.

Here's where words come in. You could use etching cream to engrave a word on the glass that is only visible up close. Or there could be writing on a tiny slip of paper (or a leaf) hidden inside the jar, a word painted on the bottom of the jar, or a stone in the jar that's been painted with a word or phrase. There are so many possibilities! You could add a decorative ribbon with writing on it, or perhaps seal the bottle with wax and stamp a word into it. If your bottle has a cork, you could write something on that as well. The paper inside could be handmade and the writing done with specially charged pen and ink. Every detail adds to the magical energy of the piece.

Here's a list of materials to consider including in your witch bottle: salt, bent nails, straight pins, thorns, one of your fingernails or a strand of hair, crystals and stones, broken glass or mirror fragments, dried herbs and flowers, any type of symbol or charm, pendants, shells, feathers, and more. This is completely up to you. Obviously, your purpose and goal will determine your choice of stones, herbs, oils, etc. These make good protection bottles to place near your home's entrance.

Word-Witch Practice
Home

Try these ideas for working with word magic in the home.

- Put words under cushions and chairs; tape a small piece of paper to the undersides of tables, desks, computer or other work area, etc.

- For pets, put words under water or food bowls, their bed, etc., or inside a collar.

- In the kitchen, consider cabinets, food containers, appliances—stick a spell on the fridge with a magnet.

- Write or paint on dishes. As an alternate method for "breaking" instead of using clay, use an old plate or cup that you can smash.

- Don't forget about mirrors, drawers, purses and wallets, lamps, jewelry boxes, etc.

- Talk (or sing) to your plants. Bury a written spell. Trace words in the dirt with a stick. Write on a leaf and bury it in the garden or a potted plant. Decorate containers and raised beds with words and symbols.

- Consider your workplace, your vehicle, and other personal spaces.

- If you sew, you can stitch words into blankets, pillows, clothing, and more.

- You can purchase leather-stamping kits or write on leather with markers or paint. I have cut up old purses and gloves to use for magical purposes; you can also find these items in resale shops. You can also write words on the inside of belts.

- If you knit, cross-stitch, or sew, find creative ways to include words in your projects. Cut up old clothes or linens and create little spell pillows or other items with hidden or visible messages.

- If you have the skill and tools, engraving metal and other objects can be a great way to engage in spell creation or making magical objects.

- Nail polish is fun to paint with. It works well on leaves, wood, bone, glass, clay, and rock. And each bottle comes with its own brush!

- Chalk can be used on a concrete front porch to write a protection spell and symbols. This is easy to hide under a welcome mat. Make it more permanent by using paint or a marker.

- The bedroom is a great place to employ relaxation words. Write *restful sleep* on a piece of paper and tuck it inside a pillowcase. You can also put items that contain words under the mattress or under the bed, in closets, in drawers, etc.

- In the bathroom, place textual spells under the sink or in the medicine cabinets. You can also carve words into a bar of soap or attach words to containers of skin-care products. Consider using phrases like *good health* or positive affirmations such as *I am healed* for medicine bottles.
- Write the words *Protect everyone within this dwelling* or *Protect all who enter here* on a piece of paper and place it under a welcome mat or entryway rug. You can stick the paper in place with tape or even write on the rug itself if you wish.
- You can write in (or on) your shoes and clothing too. And don't forget about phone cases, key rings, and other personal items.

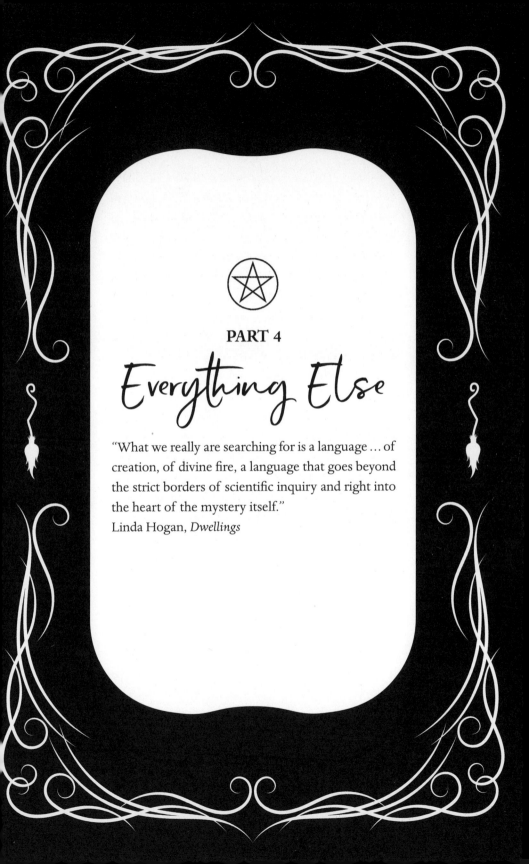

PART 4

Everything Else

"What we really are searching for is a language ... of creation, of divine fire, a language that goes beyond the strict borders of scientific inquiry and right into the heart of the mystery itself."
Linda Hogan, *Dwellings*

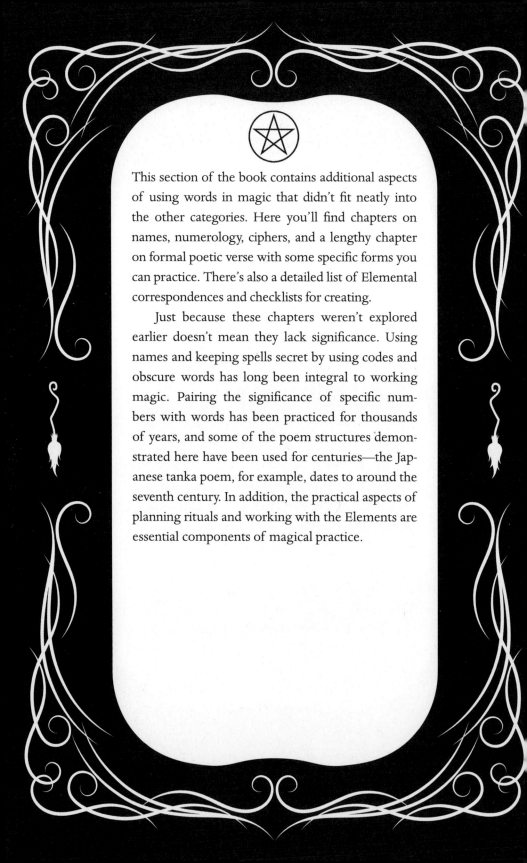

This section of the book contains additional aspects of using words in magic that didn't fit neatly into the other categories. Here you'll find chapters on names, numerology, ciphers, and a lengthy chapter on formal poetic verse with some specific forms you can practice. There's also a detailed list of Elemental correspondences and checklists for creating.

Just because these chapters weren't explored earlier doesn't mean they lack significance. Using names and keeping spells secret by using codes and obscure words has long been integral to working magic. Pairing the significance of specific numbers with words has been practiced for thousands of years, and some of the poem structures demonstrated here have been used for centuries—the Japanese tanka poem, for example, dates to around the seventh century. In addition, the practical aspects of planning rituals and working with the Elements are essential components of magical practice.

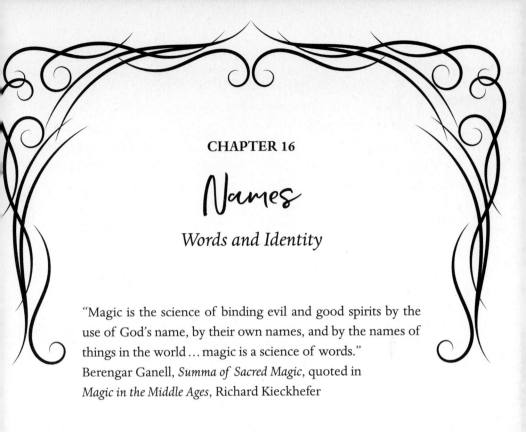

CHAPTER 16

Names

Words and Identity

"Magic is the science of binding evil and good spirits by the
use of God's name, by their own names, and by the names of
things in the world … magic is a science of words."
Berengar Ganell, *Summa of Sacred Magic*, quoted in
Magic in the Middle Ages, Richard Kieckhefer

The first uses of writing seem to have been for recordkeeping and to declare
ownership of items—especially names. Because "magic attains much of its
power by tapping into the sacred and making magical use of sacred names
and sacred narrative," some of the oldest magic involves using names, such
as invoking deity or cursing people by name.[183] Historically, the most popular
words used in magic were the names of God, the gods, spirits, saints or other
people of spiritual significance, or events. Additionally, words directed at something (an illness, for example) could be commanded "'in the name of'" or "'by
the power of'" something or someone; the power of the magic was enhanced
by an "appeal to persons, things, or events" considered sacred.[184]

Legends and stories about the importance of names can be found in folklore,
fairy tales, and myths from all around the world. Basically, many people believe
that it "tempts fate" to say certain things out loud. For example, saying the
name of something evil should be avoided because it could invoke or summon

---

183. Kieckhefer, *Magic in the Middle Ages*.

184. Kieckhefer, *Magic in the Middle Ages*.

it, or draw its attention. Saying the true name of something gives power over that thing because a "true name" reveals the nature of that thing.

In ancient Egypt, in the sacred space of a temple, reading a word inscribed on the walls was seen as potentially dangerous, especially "if it was the name of a harmful god, such as Seth, the murderer of Osiris, or the serpent Apophis who, from the distant margins of the created world, threatened the sun each morning. To prevent these divine creatures from entering the human world, the signs representing them were often scored across or stabbed with many daggers."[185]

The goddess Isis was called "'She Who Knows Everyone's Name.'"[186] There are two versions of the story of Isis gaining the knowledge of Ra's true name. One of them begins with the heat of the sun being too intense and causing harm; the other version simply implies that Ra is getting too old. In either case, Isis uses her magic to create a snake by combining Ra's spit with dirt. She places it directly in his path—the path of the sun—and it bites him. Because the snake was made using his own spit, Ra is unable to heal himself. He requests the aid of Isis (already known as a talented healer and magician), but she says she can't heal him unless she knows his true name. Eventually, he relents and tells her.[187]

Names were very important to the ancient Egyptians. Many people had both a public and private name; the private name was secret, known only to the individual and their mother.[188] According to Egyptians, "a person was made up of five parts which included two physical characteristics (his name and shadow) and three invisible elements—the *ka* (life force), the *ba* (similar to personality) and the *akh* (spirit)."[189] Basically, the name was considered an aspect of a person's soul, and as long as the name was still spoken on earth, they believed the soul would endure.[190] It was believed that damaging a person's name on their tomb was an actual attack on the deceased person's spirit. A name was more

185. Strudwick, *The Encyclopedia of Ancient Egypt*, 476.

186. Brier, *The History of Ancient Egypt*, 102.

187. Wallis Budge, "The Legend of Ra and Isis"; J. Hill, "Isis and Ra," Ancient Egypt Online, accessed July 9, 2024, https://ancientegyptonline.co.uk/isisra/.

188. Brier, *The History of Ancient Egypt*, 102.

189. Strudwick, *The Encyclopedia of Ancient Egypt*, 178.

190. *The Egyptian Book of the Dead*, 21.

than just a word, it was "an image, a representation of the being or thing to which it was attached."[191]

We all have many names—names we were given at birth, nicknames, names we've chosen for ourselves (such as Craft names, or new names to replace an undesirable birth name); performers and writers often use a stage name or pseudonym, and names are taken when people go through rites of passage, such as the Catholic confirmation or when someone takes a partner's name after getting married. We name objects too—ships have names, and some people give names to their automobiles. And of course we name our pets—and often give them cute little nicknames too. In some ways, names have become labels for our identities. They can be a source of pride or a nuisance, depending on the situation. Calling someone by a particular name or title conveys respect, but "name-calling" of a derogatory type is used to insult and cause harm.

While researching family history, I discovered that my ancestors from Finland and Germany either altered or shortened their family surnames when they came to America, as was common at the time. I also found the clan name and crest of my ancestors from Scotland. Consider doing your own research on this—you may find some surprises. It's also fun to investigate the origin of names and what they mean. You can often trace this information through your ancestors going back hundreds of years. I disliked my maiden name when I was young because (since it's Finnish) no one could pronounce it, but now I find it interesting because it links me to my heritage. And it would have been even harder to pronounce if one of my ancestors hadn't shortened it!

Names don't necessarily define us, but they can. That can be a good thing or a bad thing, depending on how you feel about your family and your specific name. And our attitude about this may change throughout our lives. When I was young, I didn't like the way my first name was spelled, and I always wanted to change it, but now I don't feel that way. I also never liked my formal first name and always went by a shortened version of it; now I like the formal name because it sounds more professional. It also seems to suit me better as I get older. And of course I have my Craft name, which has come to define me both in my magical practice and my writing career.

---

191. *The Egyptian Book of the Dead*, 161, 157.

J. R. R. Tolkien once said, "It gives me great pleasure, a good name. I always in the writing, always start with a name; give me a name and it produces a story."[192] This is an interesting approach, and it rings true on many levels: names can tell our story. We can use this in our magical practice too—not just concerning our own names, but using other names, such as calling on deities, for example.

Word-Witch Practice
Names

Here are some examples of ways to work with name magic.

- Experiment with different ways of spelling your name. Create some spellings that are secret, only known to you, and use them for special purposes.
- Create a symbol or sigil that incorporates your initials, combines all your names, or combines the letters of your name in some way.
- Writing your name on something claims ownership—use this action in spells for things you want to draw into your life. Write, carve, or etch your full name—all your names—on images of things you desire, or make a list, fold it several times, and write your name on it.
- Give something or someone a "secret" name—a pet, yourself, a loved one.
- Look around you (indoors and out) and rename things. Pretend you are seeing these things for the first time—what would you call them? Invent new names for plants, animals, automobiles—everything. Have fun with it!
- If you don't have a Craft name, choose one; have a naming ceremony or ritual.
- Invoke names to link with your ancestors. Research what your family names mean.
- Explore the use of place names in your magical practice.

---

192. J. R. R. Tolkien, "Interview," interview with Denys Gueroult, BBC Radio 4, Author Archive Collection, 1964, 39:38, June 24, 2014, https://www.bbc.co.uk/programmes/p021jx7j.

- Experiment with speaking names of deity out loud in ritual for evocation or invocation—use repetition, chanting, etc.
- There is a banishing technique in a variety of cultures of writing a person's name on a piece of paper and placing it in your shoe with the intent that repeated stepping on the name eventually "stomps" that person out of your life. Make it even more powerful by using handmade paper, ink, or both.
- Write the name of someone you want to remove from your life and cross it out. Repeat as desired. Alternately, write your name over theirs as you visualize removing their influence and suppressing their power over you.

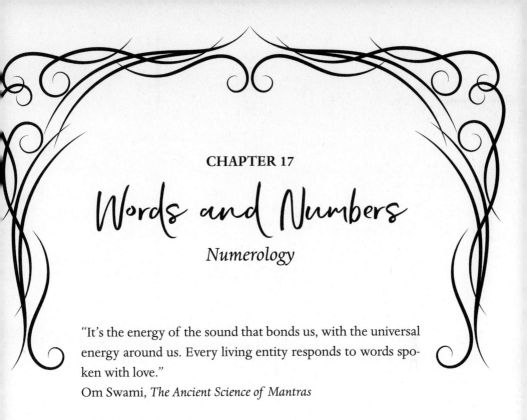

CHAPTER 17

Words and Numbers

Numerology

"It's the energy of the sound that bonds us, with the universal energy around us. Every living entity responds to words spoken with love."
Om Swami, *The Ancient Science of Mantras*

Numbers have played a role in the practice of magic for centuries. In the cases of written and spoken magic, you can use numerology to determine the number of syllables, words, or lines to create, as well as deciding the number of times to fold paper or repeat words and lines while chanting.

Numbers can correspond to letters as well, and this is called *gematria*—a way of converting letters to numerical values. This practice first appeared in ancient Greece and was eventually applied to the Hebrew and Arabic alphabets.[193] A similar technique can be applied to our alphabet in a method called the Pythagorean numerology system. You may already be familiar with this system. Each letter of the alphabet is assigned a number, 1–9. After reaching 9, repeat, starting back at 1.[194] (See also Ciphers and Codes in chapter 18.)

A	1	C	3	E	5
B	2	D	4	F	6

---

193. Miranda Lundy, *Sacred Number: The Secret Qualities of Quantities* (New York: Walker and Co., 2010), 48.

194. Michelle Arbeau, *The Energy of Words: Use the Vibration of Language to Manifest the Life You Desire* (Woodbury, MN: Llewellyn Publications, 2013), Kindle.

G	7	N	5	U	3
H	8	O	6	V	4
I	9	P	7	W	5
J	1	Q	8	X	6
K	2	R	9	Y	7
L	3	S	1	Z	8
M	4	T	2		

Add up the numbers in a word, then reduce them to a single digit. Let's look at the word *believe*. Using the system of gematria, we end up with the number 6.

B=2 + E=5 + L=3 + I=9 + E=5 + V=4 + E=5 for a total of 33; 3 + 3=6

Returning to the word *believe* as an example, in numerology, 6 is associated with creativity and balance. The positive aspect of belief includes being involved in something larger than yourself and engaging in that practice; however, there is a negative side to belief—for example, believing in something so much that one refuses to see other perspectives, causing one to be too judgmental and critical. Balance is important when using the word *believe*—the balance between remaining true to your personal convictions while leaving room to see the views of others.

Another way you can incorporate numerology is by considering the vibrations of words. In her book *The Energy of Words*, Michelle Arbeau explores this concept in depth. Building on the law of attraction—that "like attracts like"—the words we use both in magic and our mundane lives resonate in a deep way that can have profound effects—positive or negative. Arbeau also goes into detail about the "three energetic flavors" a word can have. In this case, *believe* is a 6 but also the 3 in a more subtle way. Look at the qualities of each number in the sum.[195] Within each word there is the potential for both positive and negative expressions of the energy.

You can also choose words that correspond to your birth number. Find words that vibrate to the qualities you seek and create affirmations that repeat those words. Arbeau points out that "the more a word is spoken, the more

---

195. Arbeau, *The Energy of Words*.

energy it is transmitting into your world."[196] The word is just a word—it is given life by your energy, the way you use it, and the actions you put behind it.

This list is adapted from my book *The Book of Crystal Spells,* but I've added word energy associations based on Arbeau's interpretations.[197]

One (1)

The number of solitude, permanence, unity, roots, beginning, divine spark, self-expression, ambition, and courage. Some say the number 1 has masculine energy, as opposed to 2, which has feminine energy. It's the center of the circle (the Sun), willpower, determination, leadership. Pythagoreans called it the monad—always the same, separate from the multitude. It represents the mind, is both male and female, and being added to odd makes it even and it makes the even odd. The gods Apollo and Jupiter and the goddess Vesta (hearth center) were associated with this number. One rules the sign of Leo. Sometimes just one powerful word is all you need to convey your meaning and intent. Word energy: the pioneering spirit, communication, self-expression, ego, success, new beginnings.[198]

Two (2)

Two symbolizes reflection, polarity, duality, balance, harmony of opposites, the unconscious mind, duality of humanity and the Divine, emotions, harmony, cooperation, wealth, mystery, money, marriage, feminine energy (the Moon), peace, and receptivity. The Pythagoreans considered 2 to be the duad or dyad—divided polarity. Two was associated with Isis, Diana, Ceres—mother figures. Two rules the sign of Cancer. In a grid, use 2 to represent a harmony of opposites, male and female. Or you can consider 2 symbolic of illusion (like the Moon card in tarot). You can utilize the number 2 by writing couplets. Word energy: support, the symbol of our dual nature as "spiritual beings in a physical body."[199]

---

196. Arbeau, *The Energy of Words.*

197. Grant, *The Book of Crystal Spells,* 150–55.

198. Arbeau, *The Energy of Words.*

199. Arbeau, *The Energy of Words.*

Three (3)

Three represents synthesis, movement, divinity, manifestation, trinity, creativity, joy, bridge between sky and earth, expansion, versatility, expressiveness, and luck. Pythagoreans considered this, the triad, to be the first real number. The oracles of Apollo sat upon a tripod, 3 being equilibrium, the number of knowledge and wisdom. The musical ratios of 3:2 and 3:1 are intervals of the fifth—the loveliest of harmonies aside from the octave itself. Made up of the monad and duad, the triad was sacred and was associated with the god Saturn, the goddess Hecate, the gods Pluto and Triton, and the three Fates, Furies, and Graces. The number 3 is ruled by the planet Jupiter and corresponds to the sign of Sagittarius. Repeating a word or series of words three times has long been considered powerful. Word energy: intellect—left brain; imaginative yet rational; sensitive and observant.[200]

Four (4)

Four is the number of Earth energy, the four Elements, stability, solidarity, crossroads, discipline, will, order, practicality, endurance, efficiency, materiality, and instinct. The Pythagorean tetrad was the root of all things, the perfect number. It was order, symbolic of the divine; balanced; the first geometric solid; the soul (consisting of the four powers: mind, science, opinion, and sense). Four was associated with the gods Mercury, Hercules, Vulcan, and Bacchus. The planet Uranus wasn't known in the times of Pythagoras; they associated 4 with Mercury. Four is the number of the sign of Aquarius and the planet Uranus. Word energy: practicality; the "'anchor.'"[201]

Five (5)

Five represents humanity and life itself, protection, love, reproduction, regeneration, strength, intelligence, the five senses, freedom, communication, struggle, confusion, curiosity, adventure, and sensory experiences. Pythagoreans called this the pentad—the union of odd and even, sacred symbol of light, health, and vitality. A perfect division of the perfect number 10, it also contains the fifth Element, Ether. Five is symbolic of nature (only 5 and 6 when multi-

---

200. Arbeau, *The Energy of Words*.

201. Arbeau, *The Energy of Words*.

plied by themselves end in their original number). Four plus 1, the Elements plus the monad, equals 5. The pentagram was a sacred symbol of life and associated with the goddess Venus. The planet Venus makes a fivefold pattern as it orbits the sun. We find fives everywhere in nature—even in our physical form. The associated planets are Venus and Mercury; the astrological signs of Gemini and Virgo. Word energy: expression; artistic, "'heart and soul.'"[202]

Six (6)

Six is a "perfect number" symbolizing beauty, union of conscious and unconscious minds, balance, creation, perfection, wholeness, healing, love, wisdom, responsibility, release, union of opposites, idealism, loyalty, harmony and perfection, domesticity, and truthfulness. Pythagoreans called this the hexad, and it was the creation of the world—perfection, the union of two triangles. Six is the sum and product of the first three numbers (1, 2, 3) and its factors are also 1, 2, and 3. This is one reason it's called a "perfect" number. To the Pythagoreans, it symbolized harmony, marriage, and balance (and was associated with Orpheus). Crystalline structures such as snowflakes and quartz crystals are built on the number 6, a cube has six sides, and honeycombs are hexagrams. The astrological signs associated with 6 are both Taurus and Libra. The Pythagoreans did not associate a planet or deity with 6; however, it corresponds to the planet Venus based on the signs of Taurus and Libra. Word energy: creative; links left and right brain; potential.[203]

Seven (7)

Seven represents perfect order, a mystical and sacred number, higher learning, spirituality, magic, wisdom, law, intelligence, divinity, mystery, and solitude. In Pythagorean philosophy, the heptad was the number of religion and life, fortune, judgment, dreams, and sounds. It was associated with the god Mars. Three plus 4—soul plus world—equals the mystic nature of humankind, the threefold soul or spirit (spirit, mind, and soul). There are seven chakras, seven visible colors in the spectrum, and seven days of the week—named for the

---

202. Arbeau, *The Energy of Words.*
203. Arbeau, *The Energy of Words.*

seven celestial bodies of ancient times.[204] Seven is associated with the god Osiris and the planet of Neptune (based on its association with the sign of Pisces). The planet Neptune was not known in the time of Pythagoras; they associated this number with the god Mars. The number 7 has long been regarded as a mystery number among various religious traditions. Word energy: truth; the energy of learning through experience; wisdom and knowledge.[205]

Eight (8)

Eight is the number of strength, life-force energy, discipline, eternity, authority, courage, regeneration, good luck, justice, practicality, power, salvation or spiritual evolution, retribution, balance, and material success. Pythagoreans called this *ogdoad* and it symbolized love, counsel, and the god Neptune. It was associated with the Eleusinian Mysteries. Eight was special because it could be divided into 4, then 2, and then each 2 separated back to 1. Eight corresponds to the planet Saturn and the sign of Capricorn. Word energy: leader; wise and independent; confident and assertive yet compassionate.[206]

Nine (9)

Nine represents completeness, change, achievement, culmination, order, action, physical prowess, forgiveness, compassion, inspiration, spirituality, and divine love. Pythagoreans called this ennead. It's 3 × 3, which is the first square of an odd number.[207] Nine is the first number that can be used to construct a magic square. Nine was called the "number of man" by the Pythagoreans (human gestation time is nine months).[208] But, since 9 falls short of the perfect number, 10, it symbolized horizon and boundary to the Pythagoreans. One description is that "it gather[s] all numbers within itself."[209] It was associated

---

204. For example, Thursday was named for Thor but is associated with Jupiter (Jove) because both deities have connections with thunder and lightning.

205. Arbeau, *The Energy of Words*.

206. Arbeau, *The Energy of Words*.

207. Manly P. Hall, *The Secret Teachings of All Ages*, Sacred Texts, 1928, https://sacred-texts.com/eso/sta/sta16.htm.

208. Hall, *The Secret Teachings of All Ages*.

209. Hall, *The Secret Teachings of All Ages*.

with the god Prometheus and the goddess Juno. The corresponding planet is Mars, and the sign is Aries.

There is much magic surrounding the number 9. If you add up the numbers 1–9, they equal 45, and 4 plus 5 is 9. Nine can't be destroyed no matter how many times you multiply or add it—and this is true for no other number. All products of 9 can be reduced to 9. Try it. Three times 9 is 27, and 2 plus 7 is 9. Nine times 9 is 81, and 8 plus 1 is 9. Nine times 4 is 36, and 3 plus 6 is 9. Word energy: charitable; idealistic, responsible; "seeker of peace and justice."[210]

Word-Witch Practice
Words and Numbers

Try these ideas for working with numbers.

- If you don't already have a Craft name, choose one for yourself based on numerology.
- Write chants (or rewrite some of your existing ones) and choose numbers of lines, numbers of syllables per line, or both based on numerology. For example, write a protection spell that has 5 lines with 5 syllables in each line.
- Determine the numerological energy of a key word and use it in a One-Word Spell. (See chapter 11.)
- Consider exploring how numerology is used in other cultures and ways you can combine those methods with words and letters.

---

210. Arbeau, *The Energy of Words*.

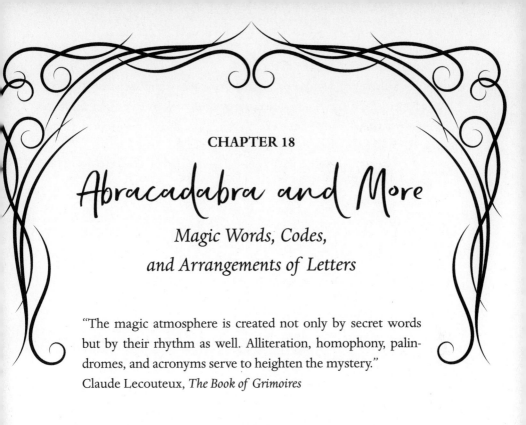

CHAPTER 18

Abracadabra and More

Magic Words, Codes, and Arrangements of Letters

"The magic atmosphere is created not only by secret words but by their rhythm as well. Alliteration, homophony, palindromes, and acronyms serve to heighten the mystery."
Claude Lecouteux, *The Book of Grimoires*

This chapter will begin with a look at some traditional magic words and then move on to explore ciphers and other special arrangements of letters that have magical uses.

Magic Words

Words like *abracadabra* have become associated with stage magic or humor but were once considered quite powerful, being magic formulae long used by ceremonial magicians. In fact, the word *abracadabra* is so well known because it's one of the most famous textual amulets.[211] Nevertheless, the word being shrouded in mystery is what makes it so interesting. It dates to the eleventh century BCE and first appeared on a Greek amulet.[212] But the style it was written in—a mode of diminishing—can be used for nearly any purpose. This is referred to as a "reductive" phrase or spell, and it was a method that could be

---

211. Several sources claim that the word *abracadabra* means "I create as I speak," but there is no solid documentation to prove this.

212. Lecouteux, *Dictionary of Ancient Magic Words and Spells*.

used for any number of words or phrases. The logic behind it is that the letters of a word are written and "subtracted one by one, with the idea that the illness will similarly shrink."[213] The basic idea is that by reducing a word, the thing it represented would also disappear. Here's an example:

ABRACADABRA

ABRACADABR

ABRACADAB

ABRACADA

ABRACAD

ABRACA

ABRAC

ABRA

ABR

AB

A

Many of the spells preserved in grimoires or artifacts sound humorous or distasteful to us today, but we can still draw on some of these for inspiration, especially if you like the idea of using a magic word that was in use centuries ago. Here are a few examples.[214]

Abraxas (or Abrasax)

Considered to be a divine name, this is one of the most common words that appear in the magical papyri from ancient Greece. This word has been found on so many amulets (mainly carved in stone) that the word *Abraxas* has "become synonymous" with the word *amulet*. It was believed this word could attract the "'intelligence of the world'" and other "'beneficial influences.'"[215] It was often accompanied by images of the sun, since Pythagoras presumed this

---

213. Lecouteux, *Traditional Magic Spells for Protection.*

214. For a deeper exploration, I recommend perusing the *Dictionary of Ancient Magic Words and Spells* by Claude Lecouteux.

215. François-André-Adrien Pluquet, quoted in Lecouteux, *Dictionary of Ancient Magic Words and Spells.*

intelligence resided there.[216] Over time, the images and symbols used with it changed and were applied to many different uses.

Merida, Meron, Mionda, Ragon

These words were believed to protect against the spells of others. The directions state that the words "must be written in large letters on paper on a Thursday before sunrise."[217] Then the paper should be hidden beneath the armpit.

Milkefe Quisen Gund Qvara Ligeami

This one was used for attracting love. The directions say to speak the words "over a pitcher of beer" and then blow on it.[218]

Ritas Ombas Zamarath

It is believed these words were used to acquire knowledge in a particular area, especially in the arts or sciences.[219]

Other Options

You can also invent your own words. You can simply come up with words using your imagination or by using the first letter or a combination of letters in a word or phrase. You can pick and choose the letters to come up with something you can pronounce. For example:

"True love find me" could be "trulofim" or "tulofime"
"Banish and be gone" could be "bagobe"

The arrangement of words in various shapes and rearrangement to obscure meaning has long been a characteristic of magic, especially amulets. Writing in the shape of a triangle was believed to be magically potent. In magical practices from ancient Greek, words arranged this way were called "wings," and the

---

216. François-André-Adrien Pluquet, quoted in Lecouteux, *Dictionary of Ancient Magic Words and Spells*.

217. Lecouteux, *Dictionary of Ancient Magic Words and Spells*.

218. Lecouteux, *Dictionary of Ancient Magic Words and Spells*.

219. Lecouteux, *Dictionary of Ancient Magic Words and Spells*.

words were typically arranged from longest to shortest—the point of the triangle at the bottom.[220]

Other Languages

While I find ancient magic words to be an interesting field of study, I don't find most of the existing words from ancient texts useful for my practice. I prefer to use words that mean something to me, but when I'm in the mood for something that sounds mystical, I prefer Latin. However, there is evidence (as mentioned in part 1) that hearing and speaking words you believe to have power can be effective even if you don't understand them. This is personal preference. If you decide to use words from another language that you don't speak, you can certainly use a dictionary. Just remember that it will be impossible to create accurate sentences without knowing the grammar. Of course, if that doesn't matter to you, that's fine. If you'd like to pursue learning a different language for magic, check out Patrick Dunn's short book on the subject: *Learning Languages for Magic*. Language is so fundamental to our lives that we take it for granted. Learning another language can help us appreciate what a wonderful invention it is. Our perspectives and worldviews can only expand as we learn more about how others communicate. Learning more about language can even change how we define reality.

Here are some other ways to play with the arrangement of letters and words:

- An *acronym* is a word made up of the first letters of several words. For example, LASER stands for "light amplification by stimulated emission of radiation." Experiment with taking existing words and making up your own acronyms. I did this in *Magical Candle Crafting* with "ME" to stand for "My Energy."[221] I'm particularly fond of author Susan Pesznecker's example, *POWER*: "Proceed Outward With Eternal Radiance."[222]

---

220. Lecouteux, *Dictionary of Ancient Magic Words and Spells*.

221. Grant, *Magical Candle Crafting*, 27.

222. Susan Pesznecker, *Crafting Magick with Pen and Ink: Learn to Write Stories, Spells and Other Magickal Works* (Woodbury, MN: Llewellyn Publications, 2009), Kindle.

- In a true *anagram*, the letters of a word (or set of words) are rearranged to spell something else—ideally, a clever relationship to the original word (or words). For example, *silent* and *listen*.
- *Palindromes* are words or phrases that read the exact same way backward and forward. The word comes from the Greek (as so many words do!) *palin* ("back" or "again") and *dromos* ("direction"). They've been used for centuries, and have been created in Latin, ancient Greek, and Sanskrit. The concept dates to around the third century BCE. One of the oldest surviving examples, the Sator square (also called a magic square, see the next page), dates to the first century CE. In English, the words *radar* (which is also an acronym) and *level* are palindromes. Phrases are harder to create: *top spot* is an example.

Try creating a palindrome-style poem or spell based on the arrangement of words—for example:

begin

and

end

unknown

becomes

known

on the journey

known

becomes

unknown

end

and

begin

Magic Square

While we typically associate a magic square with numbers, there are examples from ancient magic that incorporate words.[223] The most famous example is sometimes referred to as the "Sator square" and it was written like this:

S	A	T	O	R
A	R	E	P	O
T	E	N	E	T
O	P	E	R	A
R	O	T	A	S

The Latin words are "sator," "arepo," "tenet," "opera," and "rotas."

The arrangement here is interesting because the words can be read the same way in multiple directions. This specific arrangement has been found inscribed on stone, written on cloth (to be carried or worn), and displayed in homes for protection. References from medieval Europe indicate it was also used to ease childbirth, protect livestock, and to "win the favor of all those one met."[224] The earliest found record of it comes from the first century CE in Pompeii. There are many theories about what these words mean. One is that the letters are an anagram for "Pater Noster," which, in Latin, are the opening words of the Lord's Prayer, but this has been mostly deemed coincidence.[225]

---

223. A magic square is an arrangement of numbers that equal the same sum in all directions—rows, columns, and diagonally.

224. Kieckhefer, *Magic in the Middle Ages*.

225. Kieckhefer, *Magic in the Middle Ages*.

According to the Museum of Witchcraft and Magic, the phrase translates as "The Creator, to whom I appeal for help, controls all our endeavours and all the changes of fortune that befall us."[226] They explain it as follows:

> "Arepo" literally means "I crawl to" (it is an abbreviated form of "adrepo"); 'Tenet' means 'He holds'; 'Opera' means 'Endeavours' or 'Achievements'; 'Rotas' literally means 'Wheels', indicating the cycles of the Wheel of Fortune and the cycles of life."[227]

Others sources say it was a palindrome used to refer to a sower and his plow: "The laborer Arepo carefully guided the plow, " which is based on these translations: sower/sator; plow/arepo; tenet/holds; opera/purpose; rotas/wheels.[228] And as if these interpretations aren't enough (and there are more), "the magic square conceals the name of God. It is enough to replace the letters by their place number in the alphabet, then add together the two figures of the results." In every instance, the resulting number can be reduced to 10, which can be reduced to 1.[229]

Experiment with combinations of words to create your own magic square. It can be challenging but also rewarding. You can start by researching words and phrases that are palindromes and see how you can arrange them to make a meaning that suits your goal. If you can't find the right words in English, try another language. Another approach is to use anagrams instead of palindromes or hide specific words in a square of letters (like a word-find puzzle). You can also combine letters and numbers.

Ciphers and Codes

Back in the "old days" before texting, my childhood friends and I loved using pig Latin to write notes to each other in secret code. Although it doesn't fool anyone, it's fun. Morse code and others aren't really secret, because if everyone

226. "1583—Charm: Talisman Sator Square," Museum of Witchcraft and Magic, accessed April 18, 2024, https://museumofwitchcraftandmagic.co.uk/object/charm-talisman/.

227. "1583—Charm: Talisman Sator Square."

228. Lecouteux, *Dictionary of Ancient Magic Words and Spells.*

229. Lecouteux, *Dictionary of Ancient Magic Words and Spells.*

knows it, it can be easily deciphered. But you can create your own systems to encode your words.

In a transposition cipher, the letters of your spell or affirmation are rearranged according to a key or secret word that can be used to solve the code. One popular type is called a rail fence cipher, and there are many variations.[230]

The process of creating and decoding a message is easier if you divide the cipher into a small group of "words" that have a limited number of letters, such as four or five, per "word." This technique is optional, but useful if you want to avoid a long string of letters with no spaces between them.

While these types of codes were intended for the sending of secret messages, in this case, I'm using a phrase that I might use for spellwork: "good fortune."

Here's how to encode that phrase in case you don't want anyone to know what it is. First, count the number of letters in your message. In this case, it's eleven. Since I want to use multiples of four for my cipher, I need to add a "dummy" or "null" letter to make it so. In this case, I only need to add one to make the total twelve (the closest multiple of four). I'm going to use the letter "y."

Then write all the letters of your message and the "null" letter(s) at the end by staggering them like this:

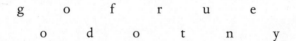

g   o   f   r   u   e
  o   d   o   t   n   y

Then write them all together, top line then bottom line: "gofrueodotny."

Because this was created using a system of four, divide the group of words into sets of four letters each: "gofr ueod onty." The use of the number four is my choice; I simply find it aesthetically pleasing to have a series of words instead of a long string of letters.

If you were using this technique to encode a secret message to someone, they could solve it by taking the string of letters (without the spaces between them) and dividing it in half (this is where choosing an even number comes in handy). Write down the first letter of the left word, then the first letter of the right half, then the second letter of each "word" and so on, ignoring the null letters at the end: "gofrue" or "odotny."

---

230. Gardner, *Codes, Ciphers, and Secret Writing*.

In a type of cipher called a substitution cipher, the order of the letters remains consistent, but each one is assigned a corresponding symbol, number, or other letter.[231] This is very popular in numerology, where the alphabet is written out and each letter is assigned a number. The Pythagorean numerology system is a type of substitution cipher, but you can create your own secret version by assigning different numbers or even symbols to the letters of the alphabet.

Another common cipher is the alphabet shift, where a second alphabet is written beneath the original one, but the letters are shifted as you choose.

A	B	C	D	E	F	G	H	I	J	K	L	M	N	O	P	Q	R	S
			A	B	C	D	E	F	G	H	I	J	K	L	M	N	O	P

So in this case, D would be A, E would be B, and so on.

Word-Witch Practice
Magic Words and Codes

Try these activities to work with magic words and codes.

- Create your own magic words and codes by rearranging letters of words and phrases. Use these new "magic" words in written spells (especially since they may end up being difficult or impossible to pronounce). These words are good choices for amulets, talismans, and curse tablets.
- If you create a word that's easy to pronounce, practice reciting it until it becomes meaningful to you. Use it in a One-Word Spell (see chapter 11).
- Try creating your own magic square with words that pertain to a spell or affirmation, and experiment with different surfaces on which to write it. (See part 3.)
- If you speak multiple languages, experiment with mixing words from each language.

---

231. Gardner, *Codes, Ciphers, and Secret Writing.*

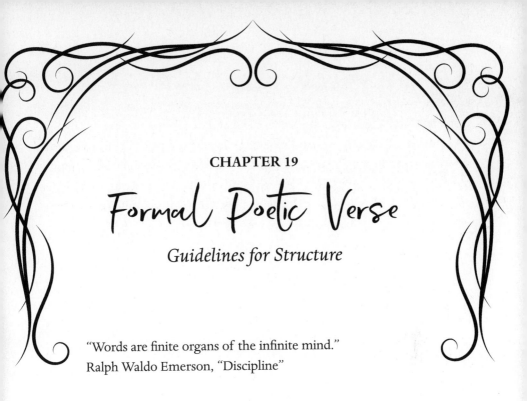

CHAPTER 19

Formal Poetic Verse

Guidelines for Structure

"Words are finite organs of the infinite mind."
Ralph Waldo Emerson, "Discipline"

Why bother with formal verse? Because some of these forms have a very pleasant rhythmic arrangement and have been used for hundreds, even thousands, of years. Some of these forms have specific rules for rhyme and number of syllables or number of lines, making them good choices for incorporating aspects of numerology. One advantage of using formal structure is that the "restrictions of form push you to be more resourceful, to find the language you need."[232] While most of the poetry I write is free verse (no specific arrangement of lines or meter), I often enjoy writing spells and other magical works with a formal structure because I enjoy the challenge. I've listed several here for you to try (but feel free to bend the rules!).

Poetic Meter

Before we look at the forms, let's address one more term: *poetic meter*. You may never end up using this in your work, but knowledge of it can be useful in creating rhythmic patterns. The discussion of meter involves another term: *foot*.

---

232. Addonizio and Laux, *The Poet's Companion*, 140.

Why the word *foot*? This goes back to poetry's early link with dance, "when each rhythmic unit was marked by a beat of the dancer's foot."[233] Poetically speaking, a foot consists of a set of stressed and unstressed syllables.

The act of scansion involves looking at a line of poetry (scanning it) to determine where the stressed and unstressed syllables are and then seeing if there's a pattern of feet. The tricky part is that when you're scanning an entire line, the words themselves don't matter. Let's use this famous first line from "Elegy Written in a Country Churchyard" by Thomas Gray (1751):

The curfew tolls the knell of parting day.[234]

I've used bold in the example below to indicate the stresses. This is *iambic pentameter*—a series of five feet called *iambs*.

The **cur** *few* **tolls** *the* **knell** *of* **part** *ing* **day**

So how do you know if a one-syllable word is stressed or unstressed? You say the line out loud and see if you can "feel" it. That's why this is not an exact science.

Here are the basic poetic feet. The ˘ symbol is used to indicate an unstressed syllable; the - symbol is a stress.

iamb: an unstressed syllable followed by a stress ˘ - (de **DUM**)

trochee: a stressed syllable followed by an unstressed one - ˘ (**DUM** de)

anapest: two unstressed followed by a stressed syllable ˘ ˘ - (de de **DUM**)

dactyl: a stressed syllable followed by two unstressed - ˘ ˘ (**DUM** de de)

pyrrhic: two unstressed syllables ˘ ˘ (de de)

spondee: two stressed syllables - - (**DUM DUM**)

Patterns are units of two (dimeter), three (trimeter), four (tetrameter), five (pentameter), six (hexameter), and so on. Iambic pentameter is probably one you've heard of if you've ever taken a literature course. This means the line contains five iambs: de **DUM**, de **DUM**, de **DUM**, de **DUM**, de **DUM**. The "de

---

233. Nims and Mason, *Western Wind*, 210.

234. Thomas Gray, "Elegy Written in a Country Churchyard," Poetry Foundation, accessed May 29, 2024, https://www.poetryfoundation.org/poems/44299/elegy-written-in-a-country-churchyard.

DUM" is like a heartbeat and is the most common and popular rhythm. Typically, in formal verse that uses this meter, there are rhymes at the ends of lines; *blank verse* is iambic pentameter that doesn't use end rhymes.

You discover the feet by first locating the stressed and unstressed syllables in a line. Then you look to see if there's a pattern (there doesn't have to be one). Here's the previous example of iambic pentameter with the feet marked. It can get confusing because feet don't matter when considering single words. A word can be divided, such as the words "curfew" and "parting."

The **cur** | few **tolls** | the **knell** | of **part** | ing **day**

For one more example, here's a line from my "Yuletide Tree Blessing":

Let **every branch** and **point** of **light**
Let **ev** | ery **branch** | and **point** | of **light**

This line is iambic tetrameter—four iambic feet.

If poetic meter doesn't interest you, that's perfectly fine. If it does, I encourage you to pursue it further.

Sonnet

There are two main types of sonnets—both styles consist of fourteen lines, but the rhyme scheme is different. Long ago they were mainly used for religious purposes, but over time they have become a classic style used by many famous poets. Remember, you should feel free to bend the "rules," but I do recommend trying to adhere to them at first, just to have the experience.

The *Italian* (or Petrarchan) has a rhyme scheme of abba abba cdd cee (or cde). The first eight lines (the octave) set up the premise of the piece, and the next six lines (the sestet) respond. The *English* (Shakespearean) is probably the more well-known of the two styles, thanks to Shakespeare. The rhyme scheme is abab cdcd efef gg. This type is organized into three sets of four (quatrains) with a couplet at the end. Line nine of the sonnet is called a *volta*, or "turn"— usually a moment of change or a turning point. Typically, a sonnet is written in iambic pentameter. Here are some examples.

This is an English (Shakespearean) sonnet from *Magical Candle Crafting*.[235]

---

235. Grant, *Magical Candle Crafting*, 102–3.

A Sonnet for the Summer Solstice

The land is soaked in light of longest day,	a
the leaves of all the trees invoke a spell—	b
the night will bring the frolic of the fae	a
and music of a foxglove's graceful bell.	b
The potent plants—verbena, rose, and rue,	c
the mythic battle that this day evokes;	d
a turning of the Wheel as ever true—	c
the Holly King defeats the King of Oak.	d
Upon the night the moon is poised to shine,	e
her silver touch turns grass to burnished blades;	f
the woods are lush with lichen, herb, and vine,	e
while wingéd magic dances in the glades.	f
We now begin the waning of the year—	g
we welcome this Midsummer night with cheer!	g

Note that I've mainly kept all the lines end-stopped here. This was written as part of a group ritual with the intent to celebrate the summer solstice, which is why I used "we." My goal was to use words that evoked images of the season and to also reference the topics of longest day and the legend of the Holly and Oak Kings. I also kept to a strict meter and rhyme here (with a few exceptions).

Here's one that was originally called "A Sonnet for the Moon" (*The Second Book of Crystal Spells*), but I have revised it.[236] Even when I use iambic pentameter, I don't always stick to it rigidly. I actually prefer to just have a pleasing sound and will add or remove a syllable if it suits my goal. This is an Italian (Petrarchan) sonnet, but I've slightly altered the rhyme scheme: abba, abba, cdc, dcd.

---

236. Grant, *The Second Book of Crystal Spells*, 182.

A Sonnet for the Moon

Tonight the moon is asking me to dance,	a
her glow descends upon the grass and stone,	b
she beckons me to walk the path alone,	b
without a question or a backward glance.	a
With moonlight as my guide I take a chance,	a
compelled to walk I enter the unknown,	b
into a forest green I deeply roam,	b
and move into a mystic kind of trance.	a
At last I pause and softly bend to kneel,	c
beneath the trees I touch the sacred ground.	d
The wisdom light and shadow soon reveal—	c
that to the universe my soul is bound.	d
By leaf and stone and moonlight I am healed,	c
the meaning that I seek is finally found.	d

A piece like this could be used as a devotional hymn or affirmation.

Villanelle

Villanelles are fun, and I always have my creative writing students try their hand at one. I like them because of the interesting rhyme scheme. These are nice to use in rituals. The *villanelle* (*villanella*) was once a type of Italian pattern used in folk songs that became a form of French verse in the sixteenth century.[237] The formula may seem confusing at first, but once you recognize the pattern, it's really quite simple. They are supposed to be songlike. Here is one of mine to use for reference. I've kept these to a fairly even meter, although that's not required.

I've noted the rhyme and line repetition format in the example below. The lowercase letters (a, b) indicate rhyme. In this case, I used slant rhyme, focusing on the consonance of the "n" sound (remember, the "rules" are more like

---

237. Nims and Mason, *Western Wind*, 314.

guidelines). The capital letters also correspond to the rhyme scheme, but these letters and numbers (A1, A2) designate the refrains that are repeated throughout. The following is a revised villanelle from *The Second Book of Crystal Spells.*[238]

A Villanelle for Samhain

A1	A time of change at summer's end—
b	the Wheel has turned, another year.
A2	We touch the night; the dance begins;
a	this hallowed eve the veil is thin.
b	We join our hands together here
A1	to usher in the summer's end,
a	and share the magic with our friends.
b	We own the dark, dispel the fear,
A2	we touch the night, the dance begins.
a	Embrace the tingling of the skin,
b	the witching hour's drawing near—
A1	a time of change at summer's end.
a	We whisper to the sky and when
b	the silver moonlight does appear—
A2	we touch the night, the dance begins.
a	In the circle now we spin,
b	making what we need appear.
A1	A time of change at summer's end,
A2	we touch the night, the dance begins.

This piece was created for a group ritual. I tried to keep a fairly even meter to allow for a chant-like feeling, even though I used enjambment instead of end-stopped lines. I wanted a formal feel for use in ritual. And I wanted the songlike quality.

---

238. Grant, *The Second Book of Crystal Spells*, 173–74

The easiest way to approach this is to come up with your two rhyming phrases first and then build the rest of the poem around those. The trick is that these two lines should not only have a relationship to each other, but also be able to stand independently. Since these two lines will be used together at the end, it may be useful to think of that first and then write the rest of the piece based on those ideas or images.

If you like the repetitive rhythm of the villanelle but want to write something shorter, try the rondel or triolet.

Rondel and Triolet

This type is derived from Old French poetry and is called the *rondel* (also roundel or rondelle; not to be confused with the rondeau). Another version is called the *triolet*, which has repetitions at the middle and at the end. Like the villanelle, the rondel is built around the repetition of entire lines that are repeated like a refrain. In a rondel, there are two quatrains (four-line stanzas) followed by either a quintet (five-line stanza) or a sestet (six-line stanza). Again, the lowercase letters refer to the rhyme scheme, and the uppercase letters and numbers refer to the rhyme and the repetition of specific lines.

A1	*Terrain and time*
B2	*have taught the trees*
b	*to mingle branches and leaves*
a	*with tangled vines*
a	*and trained them to rhyme*
b	*with the breeze.*
A1	*Terrain and time*
B2	*have taught the trees*
a	*to bend and twist, reach and climb,*
b	*to grasp the ground and cleave*
b	*the soil they need, yet lean*
a	*toward the light sublime.*
A1	*Terrain and time*
B2	*have taught the trees.*

I played with the rhyme scheme here, relying on assonance to create slant rhymes. Also, the word "cleave" means both to cling to something and to split or separate; roots of trees do both of these things. This piece was actually inspired by the woods on my property—there are lots of hills and leaning trees, several with wild grapevines twined among the branches.

An even easier version is the triolet:

A1	*I am healed—*
B2	*body, heart, mind, and soul.*
a	*This amulet will be my shield.*
A1	*I am healed.*
a	*With these words the spell is sealed.*
b	*I am whole,*
A1	*I am healed—*
B2	*body, heart, mind, and soul.*

Here's a couplet I originally had in mind to be chanted for an affirmation:

Body, heart, mind, and soul,
I am healed, I am whole.

When I decided to try it as a triolet, I separated the phrases in line two, and then I only had to add two more lines. I decided to create a chant that could be used on an amulet. While "shield" is often associated with protection, it can be a strong image for protection from illness. Since this form is short and only has two rhymes, it's easy. I also tried to keep the syllables even to create a pleasant rhythm. The goal of the spell ("I am healed") is repeated three times. When writing one of these, you may want to start there and build the rest of the words around that. As with others of this type, decide on the two refrains first—make those lines the most important, the goal. But use the other lines to reinforce your purpose, enhance your visualization, etc.

Rondelet

This one is shorter but actually more challenging due to the limit on syllables. The *rondelet* has seven lines with a rhyme scheme of AbAabbA. Lines one, three, and seven are refrains. The refrain lines are four syllables; the other lines have eight syllables. Here's one I built around the word "prosperity" to be used as a spell:

1	A	Prosperity,
2	b	please come to me; fulfill my need.
3	A	Prosperity—
4	a	I ask this with sincerity.
5	b	these words I speak will plant the seed
6	b	to grow and help me to succeed.
7	A	Prosperity.

It's quite simple, but it does the job. The word "prosperity"—the goal of the spell—is repeated three times. There's a rhyming pattern as well. Note how using enjambment gives room to play with the lines and syllables; punctuation makes a big difference here. It's actually harder to write it with all end-stopped lines.

These types of structured poems not only provide an opportunity for creating a rhythmic pattern, you can use them with numerology (number of syllables, number of lines). As with other forms that utilize a refrain, a good approach is to come up with your refrains and build the rest of the piece around those lines. Choose phrases that are significant to your goal and purpose, whether it's a prayer, spell, affirmation, etc.

Let's look at the word "prosperity" using numerology.

P=7 + R=9 + O=6 + S=1 + P=7 + E=5 + R=9 + I=9 + T=2 + Y=7 for a total of 62; 6 + 2=8

Eight is a number associated with strength, authority, and courage. Also note that the poetic form I used is built around syllables of 4 and 8. This spell could also be written on paper folded 8 times or used as part of a crystal grid using multiples of 4. In the traditional tarot, 8 is the Strength card. That could be added to the spell too, or light 8 candles, use corresponding crystals and plants, and more. This could be a simple spoken spell, part of an elaborate ritual, or somewhere in between. In the minor arcana of the tarot, eights broadly correspond to movement and progress toward goals, or they can help you examine if you are somehow being held back from moving forward or need to develop more skills. Strength and confidence can be seen here as the underlying force supporting prosperity. Of course, you could also choose a number that corresponds to 4; prosperity does have four syllables. And when I chose this word, I didn't know its number. I chose it because it had four syllables and was the key word that fulfilled the purpose.

Other key words, phrases, and actions indicated in this spell include planting a seed and the word "succeed." Visualization of the "seed" being planted would be important. What is that "seed"? A new job, a new skill, education? How is the success defined? Part of the spell might even involve planting an actual seed or burying something symbolic. If the spell is to get a raise or promotion, for example, something related to the job could be used. The words could be written on a pay stub or other special paper in addition to being spoken. You could also consult the list of Elemental correspondences for Earth and choose other tools or methods to enhance your spell.

Acrostic

An *acrostic* is a type of poem in which the first letters of each line spell out either the alphabet, a word, a name, or even a secret message.

> *Sunlight, bring*
> *To us*
> *All your*
> *Radiance*

This one is extremely short, just used as an example. Many people approach these as puzzles or mental exercises, and they can be fun, especially if you decide to spell out a phrase or use the entire alphabet.

Ode

Of Greek origin, *odes* are typically poems or songs used as tribute or praise, to celebrate or honor something or someone. Try writing an ode to a goddess or god, a plant, an animal, or a celestial object—anything that inspires you. They're often somewhat formal in their diction and tone, delivered with respect or awe. You can address the ode directly to the subject or write about it in third person. Your title doesn't have to be "Ode to..." but it can be. The point is, get emotional—give praise—write about something or someone you love or admire.

Here's one I wrote in honor of the Worm Moon. This one is "about" the moon, rather than being directed "to" it.

Worm Moon

Through the trees
she rises
briefly held by branches
bare and evergreen,

a scarred, pale stone
cradled like a pearl.

The first flowers greet her
as March confirms
rumors of spring's arrival;

sleeping things awaken
stirred to life by light.

With reflected radiance
she brings sunlight
into darkness,
so we can look
into the life-giving light
with naked eyes.

A similar poem is the elegy. An elegy is not a eulogy, or even an ode, although they can share characteristics. A *eulogy* is typically what we call the words said about someone at a funeral. An *elegy* is a poem (or song) written about the loss of someone. Both are expressions of grief and lament. You can use an elegy in a private ritual to honor a departed loved one (or someone you admire). There's no standard form.

Apostrophe

More than just a punctuation mark, an *apostrophe* as a poetic form dates back (as so many things do) to ancient Greece. This form is very similar to an ode. In ancient times, these would be performed on special occasions, usually with a somewhat formal or somber tone. Many of them begin with expressing "O"— as in "O, Artemis…" Epic poems often begin this way. The *Iliad* begins "Sing, Muse, the Wrath of Achilles."[239] Apostrophe "means 'a turning away,' that is, a turning away from the audience by a character in a play to speak to a character who is not present."[240]

In this type of piece, you address an absent person, concept, thing, or idea. The main difference from an ode is that you are addressing a subject that is not nearby or easily accessible—something you're longing or wishing for, perhaps, or hoping to find. These types of poems can be especially useful in spellwork, as you can address your goal or purpose in a more personal way. Consider personifying an abstract idea and writing "to" it.

Here's a poem that could be categorized as an apostrophe and used as a prayer. This was inspired by a somewhat famous petroglyph in the state of Washington. It's called Tsagaglalal (or Tsagiglalal), a Wishram word that means "She who watches all who are coming and going" but is often shortened to just "She Who Watches."

The Latin word *ave* means "hail" and was used by the Romans as a greeting. It could be used for meeting or parting—a welcome or farewell. It's the singular imperative of the verb *avere*, which means "to be well." This piece was intended to be a "call" or "greeting" to the goddess in all her forms.

She-Who-Watches

Ave, Maria, Hail, Mary,

Isis, Gaia, Inanna—

by all the names we know

and some we don't,

this is my prayer for all women:

---

239. Homer, *The Iliad of Homer*, Arthur Sidgwick and Robert P. Keep, eds., books 1–3 (Boston, MA: John Allyn, 1879), 1.

240. Ron Padgett, ed., *The Teachers & Writers Handbook of Poetic Forms*, 2nd ed. (New York: T & W Books, 2000), 14.

the wise and wild,

the shunned and feared, the cut and shamed—

See us—

even when we can't see you.

In canyons and cathedrals, by painted rock

and tapestry—with hymns, harps,

bells and beating drums—

Hear us

no matter where you dwell,

in groves of trees, on feet or wings,

in Heaven or in Avalon.

When we write the words,

light a candle, count

the beads—

One voice sings.

Innocent, fertile, or barren,

as one we cry, we call.

Ave.

This one is broken into five stanzas and employs the use of dashes (I'm quite fond of those) to draw emphasis and pause. And even though I don't like to capitalize words just because they're at the beginning of lines (that's a style that's somewhat outdated), I do like to use capitalization to increase the significance of a word. I've done that here with "See" "Hear" and "One" to intentionally make those words important. When reciting this, those words could be emphasized by speaking them louder than the others. In a group, you could have everyone say the phrases "See us" and "Hear us" and possibly the final "Ave"—a call to the goddess. In the printed version of this poem, I italicized that last word ("Ave") to indicate its importance as a spoken call. That word could even be repeated.

Ghazal

The *ghazal* is of Persian origin and was popular in the Middle East as far back as the seventh century. It has been used in Arabic, Urdu, and Turkish cultures. It's pronounced "guzzle" and in Arabic means something akin to flirtation or romantic speaking, which most likely explains the poem's early form of being a type of love poetry. Eventually the form became used for spiritual, mystical, and devotional expressions.[241] They are sometimes used to express pain or sorrow.

One main feature of this form is that it's a set of couplets with a repeated word. In older versions, the author would work his or her name into the last line, but that practice has fallen out of use in modern approaches. Modern writers have taken all sorts of liberties with the form—some don't even stick to the tradition of repeating a key word.

The other defining characteristic is that a ghazal is almost like a list, a grouping of associations. Each couplet could stand alone, but collectively, they tell a story or paint a complete picture of something. This works sort of like a collage of unrelated images, which when placed near each other, somehow create a whole picture even though the pieces don't seem to go together. The images jump around, but a connection remains between the separate parts (the couplets). It's about relationships, but the repeated word or phrase links them.

The form consists of five to twelve couplets (sets of two lines), and the lines are typically somewhat long. Rhyming is optional. The couplets are usually complete sentences or end-stopped expressions but, again, not always. A repeated word or phrase is used at the end of both lines of the first stanza and the second line of all the following ones (in this case, the stanza is a couplet—two lines). As with the villanelle, it may work best to decide on that first and then build the poem around it.

This is a lovely form to use when you don't want to focus on memorization but, instead, vivid statements—a wonderful form to use for prayer or even invocation or evocation. Begin by choosing a general topic or idea and write statements about that topic—but not statements that logically build in sequence; instead, jump around. There may be gaps in the logic and that's okay—that's the appeal of this type of piece. You can also bend the rules and use words that

---

241. Heather Sellers, *The Practice of Creative Writing: A Guide for Students*, 4th ed. (Boston, MA: Bedford St. Martin's Press, 2021), 446–47.

have similar sounds. One key to making this type of piece work is to repeat variations of certain words and images that nearly rhyme. For example, play with words that look alike and sound different or words that sound the same but look different—like *bee* and *be*, *sun* and *son*, or *see* and *sea*—and experiment with punctuation. Think of it like a collection or a collage. The sets of couplets build upon each other—like variations on a theme.

Here's a way to create one for magical use. For this one, I wanted to write about the moon. Note that I'm not exactly following the "rules" that each line should be a complete sentence; I play with the punctuation, making some of these couplets only one sentence.

> *For comfort we look to the sky, measure the movement of the moon.*
> *Symbol of cycles, our lives are always changing like the moon.*
>
> *Empress of the sky, known to all; once revered, and even feared.*
> *It's easy to forget that some have touched the moon.*
>
> *To renew and refresh, to remember the dark is essential,*
> *we contemplate the hidden light, the night of the new moon.*
>
> *An object of wonder and worship, in celebration and in secret,*
> *we take the time to look up, to marvel at the moon.*

The rhythm of the ghazal is created by the repetition of a specific word or phrase, but you don't have to worry about meter or syllables; just concentrate on creating sets of images about your topic.

Each stanza (set of couplets) could stand alone as a statement about the moon, but collectively they work together as an exploration of the various ways we appreciate the moonlight. Something like this could be used in ritual or as a prayer; it could be used in a group ritual with each person speaking a stanza.

A set of lines could be written for each of the year's full moons. For example:

She rises to a silent audience, greets the bony trees, lends them light

they use to claw long shadows on the snow; this is the Cold Moon.

Over fields of flowers newly opened, leaves and buds beginning to unfurl,

she gazes through the slowly warming darkness; we call her now Pink Moon.

Haiku, Tanka, and Renga

One of the most popular form poems is the *haiku*, popular in Japan beginning in the seventeenth century. Often associated with nature or seasonal images, they are now written for anything you can imagine. The haiku is actually part of a longer piece that first began with the *tanka*, a classical form from Japan that has been used for more than a thousand years. The tanka is a five-line poem with syllables arranged like this:

Line 1: 5 syllables

Line 2: 7 syllables

Line 3: 5 syllables

Line 4: 7 syllables

Line 5: 7 syllables

At some point, poets began writing tanka poems in a series called a *renga*, where one person would start the first three lines of 5, 7, 5, and then the next person would take over with the next two lines of 7, 7, and so on. The haiku was born from this practice, being the first three lines only: 5, 7, 5.

There's a style of American poetry that may have been inspired by the tanka—the cinquain. It has five lines with the following number of syllables: 2, 4, 6, 8, 2. These forms are all simple and fun to create.

I remember when I was an undergrad, I had a poetry class where the instructor started a tanka chain at the beginning of the semester and we kept it going, each student in the class taking our turn adding lines, all the way until the end of the semester. This type of sharing can be done for a ritual among a group and is a fun way to create a group chant or other piece to be shared.

Here are examples of how haiku and tanka can be used to create a prayer:

Goddess bring us rain,
nurture all our land and crops,
quench our drying world.

Goddess bring us rain,
nurture all our land and crops,
quench our drying world.
Well and river need to run.
Field and forest need to drink.

In the first example (haiku), to make a rhythmic chant, you could use the same first line as the last line. In the second example (tanka), you could write a refrain to serve the last two lines of the piece. Like this:

Goddess bring us rain,
nurture all our land and crops,
quench our drying world.
We all need life-giving rain.
We all need life-giving rain.

These types of poems don't typically rhyme, but you can do that if you wish, especially if you intend to use these as chants.

Formal poetic structure can be a great start to writing or a way to challenge yourself by trying something new. Just remember that these are guidelines—feel free to break the rules in the name of style.

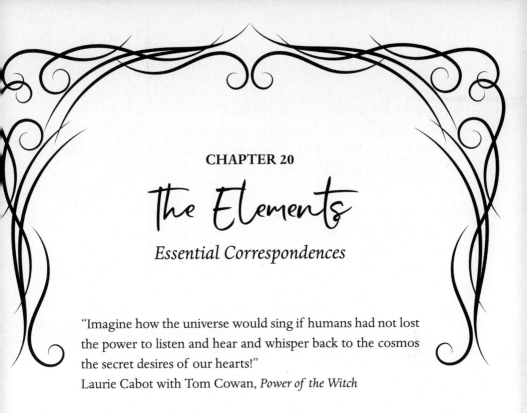

CHAPTER 20

The Elements

Essential Correspondences

"Imagine how the universe would sing if humans had not lost the power to listen and hear and whisper back to the cosmos the secret desires of our hearts!"
Laurie Cabot with Tom Cowan, *Power of the Witch*

The classical Elements of Earth, Air, Fire, and Water are an essential aspect of spell crafting. We are literally part of our cosmos, and these Elements, broadly speaking, are part of everything, connecting us to the universe. Therefore, I always capitalize them when I refer to them in this way (as opposed to their mundane counterparts). As Elements (capital E) they represent more than merely substances—they each have a distinct personality and govern the variety of purposes and practices in magic as well as all facets of our lives.

Most of our modern spells, like magical work of centuries ago, are based on various correspondences—timing, astrological influences, and associated herbs, stones, and other materials. I'm a fan of starting with the Element(s) that best correspond(s) with my purpose, and then choosing timing and materials from there. A consideration of the appropriate Element can also help you decide what to write *with* and what to write *on*. If you're uncertain how to approach your goal, consider using this as a guide. Since all the Elements can be both creative and destructive, and there can be overlap between some of their qualities, let your intuition guide your choice; most spells involve a combination of Elements.

Air

Air is probably the Element that is most obviously associated with word magic—you use air to speak, and writing involves the intellect, the mind, and creativity. It is projective and the most useful Element when speaking aloud or writing. The Taschen Library of Esoterica describes it this way: "The voice is made of air, as is language ... it transmits secret knowledge through words and whispers. Air entrances through incantation, sound waves, and song."[242]

The specific qualities of the Air Element include movement, flight, freshness, intelligence, sound, smell, the thought process and intellect, creative ideas, new beginnings, communication, spirit, psychic work, and consciousness. Use the Air Element in rituals and spells for travel, instruction, study, freedom, knowledge, and recovering lost items.

> **Methods and materials:** divination, concentration, visualization, wind magic, tossing, fanning, speaking aloud (also singing, chanting, whistling)
>
> **Elemental combinations:** Writing on a leaf and releasing it on the wind combines Air and Earth; releasing ashes of something you've burned combines Air with Fire and Earth. Depositing the ashes in water incorporates all the Elements. The wind blowing away a message in dirt, sand, or salt combines both Air and Earth.
>
> **Senses:** hearing and smell
>
> **Direction:** east
>
> **Time:** dawn, spring
>
> **Colors:** white, yellow, all pastels
>
> **Symbols:** circle, birds, clouds, eggs, feathers, incense smoke, fragrant flowers
>
> **Tools:** sword, wand, staff, broom, censer
>
> **Instruments and sounds:** flutes, bells, pipes, wind instruments
>
> **Places:** sky, clouds, mountaintops, windy places
>
> **Life cycle:** birth, initiation

---

242. *Witchcraft*, Jessica Hundley and Pam Grossman, eds., The Library of Esoterica, vol. 3 (Cologne, Germany: Taschen, 2021), 232.

Celestial bodies: Mercury, Jupiter

Energy: projective

Zodiac: Gemini, Libra, Aquarius

Earth

Following Air, Earth is probably the Element most related to word magic, especially writing, carving, or etching something. Its qualities are fertile, moist, nurturing, stabilizing, and grounding, and it governs the body, health, manifestation, and all things mundane. Use Earth in rituals and spells for money, prosperity, fertility, stability, grounding, employment, and gardening; use it for magic involving images, stones, bones, trees (and plant materials in general), knots, and binding. The act of storytelling can also be linked to the Earth Element.

Methods and materials: planting, magnets, bones, burying, creating images and words in or on soil, clay, salt, wood, fabrics and leather, or sand and paper; writing on stone or in ash, dirt, sand, or salt; engraving wood; etching glass; writing on natural fabrics, bones, or plant materials; spelling out a word or phrase with stones

Elemental combinations: Burying the ashes of something you've burned also utilizes Fire; working with ceramics and clay incorporates all Elements—clay is Earth and Water, but adding Air or Fire dries it out. (Then you can either keep the piece you create, break it, burn it, bury it, or sink it into water.)

Sense: touch

Direction: north

Time: winter, midnight

Colors: brown, green, black

Symbols: pentacle, square, earth

Tools: cornucopia, wheat, acorns

Instruments and sounds: drums, bones, any percussion

Places: caverns, woods, gardens, fertile fields

Life cycle: death, rebirth

Celestial bodies: Venus, Saturn

Energy: receptive; we often think of Earth as the Element we use for planting—nurturing things we'd like to grow. But it can also be useful for burying things to get closure or to gently remove something from our lives.

Zodiac: Taurus, Virgo, Capricorn

Fire

The qualities of Fire are purifying, destructive, cleansing, energetic, sexual, forceful, passionate, and willful; it governs strength and transformative energy of all types. Utilize the characteristics of Fire in rituals and spells for protection, courage, sexual passion, strength, authority, and banishing.

Methods and materials: any type of heat or burning—candles, sun, and storm magic

Elemental combinations: Combining a burning spell with words (Air) gives it an added boost. Carving into a candle or burning something you've written or engraved on paper, wood, foil, fabric, etc. combines Fire with Earth. If you engrave a candle and float it on water, this utilizes all Elements (glass is typically associated with Earth but also Fire, considering how glass is created); add water to a fire to make smoke or steam (all Elements). Using your own blood or the sap of trees also corresponds to Fire—these are fluids of life energy.

Sense: sight

Direction: south

Time: noon, summer

Colors: red, orange, gold, white

Symbols: flames, triangle, censer

Tools: athame, censer, wand

Instruments and sounds: all strings

Places: hearths, deserts, volcanoes

Life cycle: fruition, consummation

Celestial bodies: Sun, Mars, Jupiter

Energy: projective; a wonderful way to forcefully send out energy to the universe

Zodiac: Aries, Leo, Sagittarius

Water

The qualities of the Water Element are flowing, purifying, healing, soothing, and loving, and it governs emotions, intuition, feelings, mysteries, healing, and nurturing. Use Water in rituals and spells for purification and cleansing, bathing and showering, love, psychic awareness, dreams, sleep, peace, marriage, and friendship.

Methods and materials: anything involving water, including ice, snow, fog, and steam; also mirrors, magnets, and acts of dilution and cleansing

Elemental combinations: Water can be utilized by depositing something in a body of water, such as ashes or a rock (Earth) or floating something on the water such as a leaf or piece of paper (Earth). Using water, ink, or oils to "paint" an object can also be related to Water. Water can be used to wash something away—such as a message written in sand. Mirror magic is typically associated with Water but also Earth and Fire (considering the materials used to make the mirror). Writing on a shell can be Water magic, but shells can also be linked to the Earth Element considering the minerals of which they're composed.

Sense: taste

Direction: west

Time: twilight, autumn

Colors: all shades of blue, aquamarine, gray, shades of purple

Symbols: waning crescent moon, shells, cauldron

Tools: chalice, cauldron

Instruments and sounds: rattle, rainstick, cymbal, metal, bell

Places: oceans, rivers, sacred wells, springs

Life cycle: repose, rejuvenation

Celestial bodies: Moon, Venus, Neptune

Energy: Water is receptive; its qualities, however, have the added benefit of cleansing and renewing.

Zodiac: Cancer, Scorpio, Pisces

Other Considerations:

Projective magic involves directing energy into an object or outward, to the universe. Receptive magic is drawing energy toward you. Where is the action or change taking place? Is it within you, personally, or outside you? Many spell goals contain aspects of both in cooperation. For example, to attract a love interest, put your intent out into the world (projective), and at the same time, open yourself to receiving love (receptive), and physically get out there and meet people. This involves both internal and external magic. Another example is banishing a bad habit—send out the intent to be rid of the habit (projective), but do whatever you can to personally make change (receptive) in your life.

Does what you're doing also affect others? (For example, regarding protection—you are protecting yourself, but also creating a barrier or shield against those who would cause you harm.) A shield protects and repels, so for a protection spell it would be wise to incorporate both receptive and projective energy. Another example involves attracting general good fortune. You draw this quality to yourself but also send out your intent. Stating your goal to the universe affirms your goal and is also a type of projection. However, the other spell action you take should be receptive, drawing good fortune to you.

In a magic circle, we raise energy in a variety of ways and release it toward an intended goal. The approach I'm suggesting here is a bit more fine-tuned. If you consider the energy you're raising being directed out to the universe, to yourself, or to an object, it can change your approach and visualization. Let's say you want to charge an amulet. You can visualize the energy you raise being projected into that object, empowering it. Or you may hold the object and visualize drawing energy from the universe into it. Other methods include placing the object in sunlight or moonlight for charging. There's no wrong way to do these things, but you need to be sure you have a clear understanding of your process and method to ensure the most focused visualization technique.

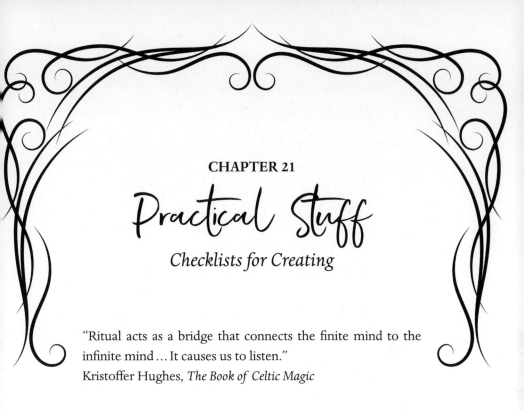

CHAPTER 21

Practical Stuff

Checklists for Creating

"Ritual acts as a bridge that connects the finite mind to the infinite mind … It causes us to listen."
Kristoffer Hughes, *The Book of Celtic Magic*

All these actions—the spells, prayers, affirmations, blessings, and rituals—keep us active in the sacred relationship we have with our world. The universe is alive with energy, and our connection with that energy is at the core of magical practice. You may not always need (or want) a formal ritual or spell to engage with this energy, but participating in this way is like a conversation with the universe and yourself, whether it's planned and formal or spontaneous. However, there is something satisfying about the creation of a meaningful ritual, a heartfelt prayer, an elegant poem. The effort you put into creating these things is part of the magic.

You can use these checklists and templates as guides for creating spells, affirmations, prayers, and rituals. In part 2, we discussed the differences between these types of expressions, and they can be either written or spoken aloud.

Getting Started

Here's a list of questions to explore that may help determine your approach.

- What is your purpose and goal? Do you need to be specific or general? Is it concrete (a particular object or thing) or abstract (a concept like love or inspiration)? Revisit the list in part 2: Are you creating a spell, ritual, prayer, affirmation, etc.?

- Is there a specific Element associated with your goal? See the list of correspondences in chapter 20 and look for associations that apply.

- Are you creating an object (talisman, amulet), taking action (lighting candles), or both?

- Are you drawing something to you, or projecting something outward to another person or to the universe to affect change, or sending something away (banishing, binding)? Sometimes you need to address an issue from both sides—banish unwanted energy while also attracting peace, or banish a bad habit while drawing strength and conviction to achieve your goal, such as removing illness and increasing good health.

- Do you desire something you can wear or carry? Do you want it to be visible or hidden? In either case, an amulet or talisman would be appropriate.

- Does the issue affect a particular part of the body, or is there a bodily association? If so, consider words on the body (tattoos, clothing, jewelry), or spells you can consume (edible paper and inks).

- Does the spell or object need to be permanent or impermanent? Permanence is best for things that need to endure—a protection spell on your home, for example—and using glass, stone, or metal would be appropriate. If it's an issue related to home and family, consider how to use word magic in your environment (indoors, outdoors, or both). Impermanence is useful for things you want to be rid of or forget, or spells that utilize a particular Element (wind or water). You can also use impermanence for spells that only need to be active for a limited time. If you're seeking a new job, for example, you might use a temporary tattoo that disappears.

- If destroying the object is part of the spell—if you really need to visualize being rid of something—consider burning or breaking something, then flushing or burying the pieces, depending on the substance. You can use wax, clay, curse tablets, wood, or paper. If the goal requires a gentler approach—letting something be carried away or removing something slowly—consider wind and water, burying, or freezing.

- What are some key words that describe your goal: *nurture, cleanse, heal, empower, banish, protect*—can you narrow it down to a word? That can help you determine your approach.

Prayers and Blessings

Here are some tips for creating prayers and blessings to help you achieve a deeper level of specificity and effectiveness.

- To whom are you speaking? One specific deity or a group? Be sure to use names or, if you prefer, Great Spirit or the Universe.
- Are you asking for something in particular? Be specific.
- Is your intent to express thanks or to offer praise? To whom? For what?
- Is the prayer or blessing for yourself or someone else?
- Is this a private expression—just you speaking to the Divine—or public, such as part of a ritual or other gathering? This will determine your tone—casual or formal—and structure. For example, is someone leading the prayer, and will there be a call and response? (See Ritual Design Template on page 216.)

Spells

Use this list as a guide for creating spells.

- Goal and purpose: This is the most important thing. It must be specific.
- Timing: time of day, season, day of week, moon phase and sign or sun sign, planetary locations, duration of spell, etc.
- Materials: crystals, candles, herbs, oils, etc. that may be determined by action.
- Tools: It's your choice if you need an elaborate altar or not—tools include wand, censer, athame, etc. Again, this may be determined by the spell action.
- Colors and symbols: any associated colors, such as candles, altar cloth, etc., or symbols you need to include—statues, sigils, etc.

- Elements: Associated Elements can play a huge role in your spell design. This can determine the action, timing, etc.
- Words: Spoken, written, or both. Is the act of writing part of the spell? The rest of this book will guide you in this process.

Ritual Design Template

These are traditional Wiccan ritual components. Each of these presents an opportunity for speaking, writing, or both. Purification of self and space is important, but the specifics of preparation for ritual are personal choice. Sometimes a personal chant or affirmation can help you focus.

- Casting the circle typically involves some form of calling the quarters/ Elementals. You can get creative here with various ways to do this.
- Invocation, if desired, is calling upon deity to be present. Again, this is a wonderful opportunity for prayer, invocation, or evocation.
- The subject of the ritual should be specifically articulated. What's your purpose? Celebrating a sabbat or esbat? Spellwork?
- The central activity of the rituals could be raising energy, spellwork, or both. This is definitely a good time to chant something or take symbolic action.
- When the central activity is complete, grounding takes place. This is another opportunity for chanting. The goal is to be sure all remaining energy is released.
- Give thanks and make an offering. This is another good chance for prayer or hymn.
- Finally, close the circle. This is not a dismissal but closure, a time to formally announce you're done.

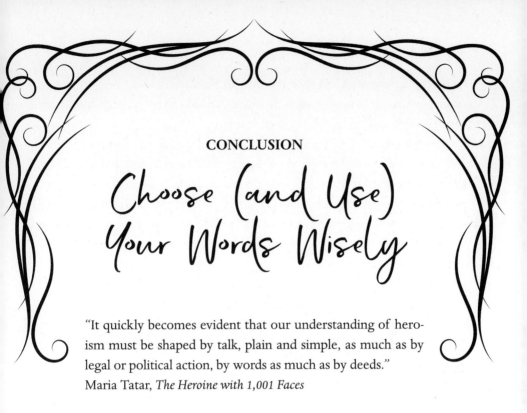

CONCLUSION

Choose (and Use) Your Words Wisely

"It quickly becomes evident that our understanding of heroism must be shaped by talk, plain and simple, as much as by legal or political action, by words as much as by deeds."
Maria Tatar, *The Heroine with 1,001 Faces*

Having a voice in this word is a valuable asset; unfortunately, not everyone has this privilege. The ability to share an opinion or speak out about injustices is precious. And while it may seem like mere entertainment, the voices of storytellers are essential as well, sharing generations of wisdom and traditions with all those who listen. To make meaning with words and communicate with others is a gift. Don't take it for granted.

There may be times when words aren't enough, when you truly feel you're at a loss for words, or the right words don't seem to exist. It happens to all of us. We don't always need words. But when we do, choosing them with intent is essential. I hope some of the ideas explored here will not only give your magical practice a boost of creativity, but also provide an opportunity to consider the impact of the written and spoken word.

Writing and language continue to evolve and change all around us. Until such time as we transcend the need for spoken or written words (assuming such things are possible), we'll keep borrowing words, changing how we say things, and developing new technologies. We've already reached the point where AI programs can write for us. While there may be some use for such things, these programs can take the human personality and thought process out of our work. No matter what the future of writing holds, keep using your personal, authentic voice. It's a powerful tool.

Remember, none of these skills matter without intent. You must mean every word you say and write. Words based on a foundation of intent and supported with materials that help you focus can create truly powerful magic. And even though this book is filled with ideas and techniques to try, they are merely suggestions. Above all, no matter how you choose to speak or write, sincere words spoken from a place of truth and genuine need that are authentically "you" are always the best choice.

Former United States poet laureate Joy Harjo once said, "To speak is to form breath and to make manifest sound into the world. As I write I create myself again and again. Re-create. And breathe."[243] This statement encompasses so much about the magic of words, both written and spoken. With the sacred breath of life, we create as we speak. And as we write, we record these moments on which to reflect. Over and over again, as we grow and change throughout our lives, we re-create our identity, express ourselves, and renew our relationships to our world and others by using words. This process is ongoing and essential. It's magic. Breathe. Write. Create. Repeat.

---

243. Robert Johnson, "Inspired Lines: Reading Joy Harjo's Prose Poems," *American Indian Quarterly* 23, no. 3/4 (Summer-Autumn 1999): 13–23, https://doi.org/10.2307/1185826.

The Words of the Witch

The words of the witch give shape and sound to magic,

are clever yet careful, confident and wise.

The words of the witch can heal and protect,

call for justice when needed, and conjure the wonder

that opens our eyes to new things. Carried

by the breath of life, expressed with sincerity and intent,

the words of the witch can create and transform,

enlighten and empower. Whether a whisper or a shout,

chanting or crying out in grief or joy, in kindness or support,

the words of the witch resonate with all of nature;

an echo from the past, new voices for the future

to inspire and express identity and desire.

The words of the witch sing in harmony with the world.

Magical Alphabets

There are many alphabets that have been created to preserve secrets of magic and ritual; some of these haven't even been deciphered.[244] Many of the most popular magical alphabets are simply substitution ciphers. Scripts such as Ogham and Nordic runes are not included here because their characters are not equivalent to modern English.

You can write words in your own language using a different alphabet and create something that seems very mystical. Or you can invent your own secret, personal alphabet. For an extensive list of magical alphabets, I recommend *The Magician's Companion* by Bill Whitcomb.

One way you can utilize secret codes and characters is by using fonts on your computer. While the majority of writing I've discussed here is done by hand, it's fun to make your digital writing pretty by using different fonts—you can even find magical alphabet fonts online. When you're reading or reciting printed text, it's nice if it "looks magical" to the eye. This is also nice if you're providing printed scripts for a group ritual. I spent lots of time on my digital

---

244. Lecouteux, *The Book of Grimoires*.

Book of Shadows years ago—special fonts, colors, images, symbols—it's truly beautiful and feels very magical. I also added pieces written by hand and some things created by stamping. This combination of formats is my favorite. I love playing with fonts to make the things I've written look lovely, and I often do this for spells I want to keep in written form that are intended to be recited.

Theban Alphabet

This writing system is a type of substitution cipher that is believed to have been developed in the sixteenth century. Some call it the "witches' alphabet" due to its history of occult use as an alternative to Latin.

A	♈	J	♈	S	♈
B	♈	K	♈	T	♈
C	♈	L	♈	U	♈
D	♈	M	♈	V	♈
E	♈	N	♈	W	♈
F	♈	O	♈	X	♈
G	♈	P	♈	Y	♈
H	♈	Q	♈	Z	♈
I	♈	R	♈		

Daggers Alphabet

This alphabet was developed by Aleister Crowley and is also a substitution cipher.

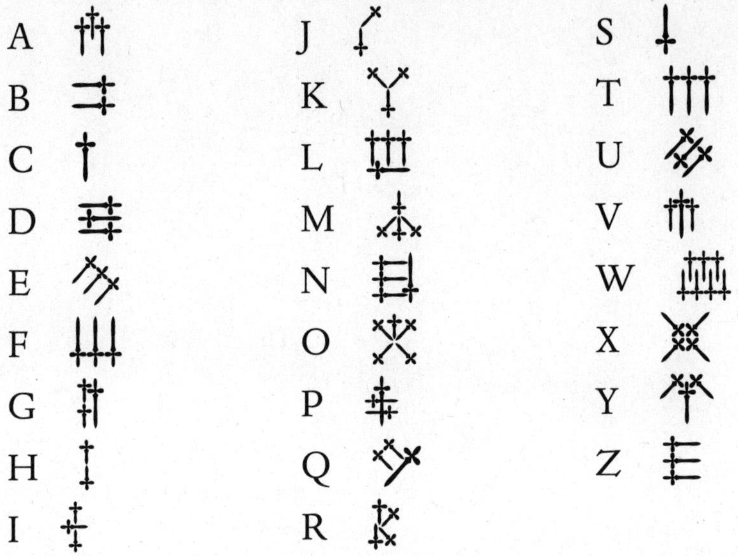

A

B

C

D

E

F

G

H

I

J

K

L

M

N

O

P

Q

R

S

T

U

V

W

X

Y

Z

Bibliography

"1583—Charm: Talisman Sator Square." Museum of Witchcraft and Magic. Accessed April 18, 2024. https://museumofwitchcraftandmagic.co.uk /object/charm-talisman/.

A History of Magic, Witchcraft and the Occult. Edited by Kathryn Hennessy. London: Penguin Random House, 2020.

Addonizio, Kim, and Dorianne Laux. *The Poet's Companion: A Guide to the Pleasures of Writing Poetry.* New York: W. W. Norton and Co., 1997.

Arbeau, Michelle. *The Energy of Words: Use the Vibration of Language to Manifest the Life You Desire.* Woodbury, MN: Llewellyn Publications, 2013. Kindle.

Askvik, Eva Ose, F. R. (Ruud) van der Weel, and Audrey L. H. van der Meer. "The Importance of Cursive Handwriting over Typewriting for Learning in the Classroom: A High-Density EEG Study of 12-Year-Old Children and Young Adults." *Frontiers in Psychology* 11 (July 2020), https://www .frontiersin.org/articles/10.3389/fpsyg.2020.01810/full.

Barrette, Elizabeth. *Composing Magic: How to Create Magical Spells, Rituals, Blessings, Chants, and Prayers.* Franklin Lakes, NJ: New Page Books, 2007. Kindle.

Bergland, Christopher. "4 Reasons Writing Things Down on Paper Still Reigns Supreme." Psychology Today. March 19, 2021. https://www.psychology today.com/us/blog/the-athletes-way/202103/4-reasons-writing-things -down-paper-still-reigns-supreme.

Betz, Hans Dieter, ed. *The Greek Magical Papyri in Translation*. 2nd ed. Chicago: University of Chicago Press, 1992.

Brier, Bob. *The History of Ancient Egypt*. Chantilly, VA: The Great Courses, 1999.

Budge, E. A. Wallis. "The Legend of Ra and Isis." In *The Book of the Dead: The Papyrus of Ani*. Sacred Texts. 1895. https://www.sacred-texts.com/egy /ebod/ebod07.htm.

Caesar, Julius. "Veni, Vidi, Vici." Oxford Learner's Dictionaries. Accessed May 24, 2024. https://www.oxfordlearnersdictionaries.com/us/definition /english/veni-vidi-vici.

Cepelewicz, Jordana. "The Brain Processes Speech in Parallel with Other Sounds." *Quanta Magazine*. October 21, 2021. https://www.quanta magazine.org/the-brain-processes-speech-in-parallel-with-other-sounds -20211021/.

"Charm." Etymology Online. Accessed May 20, 2024. https://www .etymonline.com/word/charm#etymonline_v_8449.

Cohen, Jennie. "A Brief History of Penmanship on National Handwriting Day." History. Updated May 16, 2023. https://www.history.com /news/a-brief-history-of-penmanship-on-national-handwriting-day.

Colino, Stacey. "The Case for Talking to Your Houseplants." *The Washington Post*. January 11, 2023. https://www.washingtonpost.com/home/2023 /01/11/talking-to-plants-grow-thrive/.

Crawford, Jackson. *Norse Mythology*. Chantilly, VA: The Teaching Company, 2021.

Cunningham, Scott. *Cunningham's Encyclopedia of Magical Herbs*. St. Paul, MN: Llewellyn Publications, 1999.

Curzan, Anne. *The Secret Life of Words and Their Origins*. Chantilly, VA: The Teaching Company, 2012.

David, Rosalie. *Handbook to Life in Ancient Egypt*. Revised edition. New York: Facts on File, 2003.

Davies, Owen. *Grimoires: A History of Magic Books*. New York: Oxford University Press, 2009. Kindle.

"Disguise." Cambridge English Dictionary. Cambridge University Press & Assessment. Accessed July 16, 2024. https://dictionary.cambridge.org/us/dictionary/english/disguise.

Dowling, Stephen. "The Cheap Pen That Changed Writing Forever." BBC Future. October 29, 2020. https://www.bbc.com/future/article/20201028-history-of-the-ballpoint-pen.

Drew, A. J. *A Wiccan Formulary and Herbal*. Franklin Lakes, NJ: New Page Books, 2005.

Dunn, Patrick. *Learning Languages for Magic: A Handbook to the Study of Languages for the Occult Practitioner*. Self-published, 2016. Kindle.

———. *Magic, Power, Language, and Symbol: A Magician's Exploration of Linguistics*. Woodbury, MN: Llewellyn Publications, 2008. Kindle.

The Egyptian Book of the Dead: The Book of Going Forth by Day: The Complete Papyrus of Ani Featuring Integrated Text and Full-Color Images. Revised edition. Ogden Goelet Jr., Daniel Gunther, Carol A. R. Andrews, James Wasserman, and Raymond O. Faulkner. San Francisco: Chronicle Books, 2015.

Encyclopaedia Britannica: A New Survey of Universal Knowledge. Vol. 21: Sordello to Textile Printing. London: Encyclopaedia Britannica, Ltd., 1929.

Faraone, Christopher A. "The Agonistic Context of Early Greek Binding Spells." In *Magika Hiera: Ancient Greek Magic and Religion*, edited by Christopher A. Faraone and Dirk Obbink. New York: Oxford University Press, 1991.

Gager, John G. *Curse Tablets and Binding Spells from the Ancient World*. New York: Oxford University Press, 1992.

Gandhi, Lakshmi. "Unmasking the Meaning and Marital Disputes behind Mumbo Jumbo." *NPR*. May 31, 2014. https://www.npr.org/sections/codeswitch/2014/05/31/317442320/unmasking-the-meaning-and-marital-disputes-behind-mumbo-jumbo.

Gardner, Martin. *Codes, Ciphers, and Secret Writing*. New York: Dover Publications, Inc., 1972. Kindle.

Gilbert, Robert Andrew, and John F. M. Middleton. "History of Magic in Western Worldviews." Encyclopedia Britannica. Updated May 3, 2024. https://www.britannica.com/topic/magic-supernatural-phenomenon/History-of-magic-in-Western-worldviews.

Gillett, Roy. *The Secret Language of Astrology: The Illustrated Key to Unlocking the Secrets of the Stars*. London: Watkins Media Limited, 2011.

Grant, Ember. *The Book of Crystal Spells: Magical Uses for Stones, Crystals, Minerals ... and Even Sand*. Woodbury, MN: Llewellyn Publications, 2013.

———. *Magical Candle Crafting: Create Your Own Candles for Spells & Rituals*. Woodbury, MN: Llewellyn Publications, 2011.

———. "The Three 'R's' of Chant Writing: Rhyme, Rhythm, and Repetition." In *Llewellyn's 2012 Magical Almanac: Practical Magic for Everyday Living*. Woodbury, MN: Llewellyn Worldwide, 2012.

———. *The Second Book of Crystal Spells: More Magical Uses for Stones, Crystals, Minerals ... Even Salt*. Woodbury, MN: Llewellyn Publications, 2016.

Gray, Thomas. "Elegy Written in a Country Churchyard." Poetry Foundation. Accessed May 29, 2024. https://www.poetryfoundation.org/poems/44299/elegy-written-in-a-country-churchyard.

Gottschling Huber, Beth. "Don't Write Off Cursive Yet." National Museum of American History. February 24, 2022. https://americanhistory.si.edu/blog/cursive.

"Guise." Cambridge English Dictionary. Cambridge University Press & Assessment. Accessed July 16, 2024. https://dictionary.cambridge.org/us/dictionary/english/guise.

Hale, John R. *Exploring the Roots of Religion*. Chantilly, VA: The Teaching Company, 2009.

Hall, Manly P. *The Secret Teachings of All Ages*. Sacred Texts, 1928. https://sacred-texts.com/eso/sta/sta16.htm.

Hamilton, Jon. "Scientists Find Speech and Music Live on Opposite Sides of the Brain." NPR. February 27, 2020. https://www.npr.org/2020/02/27/810095481/scientists-find-speech-and-music-live-on-opposite-sides-of-the-brain.

Hartley, Cecil. *Principles of Punctuation: or, The Art of Pointing*. Effingham Wilson, 1818.

Hill, J. "Isis and Ra." Ancient Egypt Online. Accessed July 9, 2024. https://ancientegyptonline.co.uk/isisra/.

Homer. *The Iliad of Homer*. Edited by Arthur Sidgwick and Robert P. Keep. Books 1–3. Boston, MA: John Allyn, 1879.

Hutton, Ronald. *Queens of the Wild: Pagan Goddesses in Christian Europe: An Investigation*. New Haven: Yale University Press, 2022. Kindle.

———. *The Witch: A History of Fear, from Ancient Times to the Present*. New Haven, CT: Yale University Press, 2017. Kindle.

"Incantation." Merriam-Webster. Accessed May 20, 2024. https://www.merriam-webster.com/dictionary/incantation.

Jay, Timothy. "The Utility and Ubiquity of Taboo Words." *Perspectives on Psychological Science* 4, no. 2 (March 2009): 153–161, https://doi.org/10.1111/j.1745-6924.2009.01115.x.

Johnson, Robert. "Inspired Lines: Reading Joy Harjo's Prose Poems," *American Indian Quarterly* 23, no. 3/4 (Summer-Autumn 1999): 13–23, https://doi.org/10.2307/1185826.

Judith, Anodea. *Chakra Balancing: A Guide to Healing and Awakening Your Energy Body*. Boulder, CO: Sounds True, 2004.

Kieckhefer, Richard. *Magic in the Middle Ages*. 3rd ed. Cambridge, UK: Cambridge University Press, 2022. Kindle.

King, Hobart M. "Chalk" Geology.com. Accessed April 12, 2024. https://geology.com/rocks/chalk.shtml.

Kivelson, Valerie A. and Christine D. Worobec, eds. *Witchcraft in Russia and Ukraine, 1000–1900: A Sourcebook*. Ithaca, NY and London: Northern Illinois University Press, 2020. Kindle.

Landon, Brooks. *Building Great Sentences: How to Write the Kinds of Sentences You Love to Read*. New York: Penguin, 2013.

Lecouteux, Claude. *The Book of Grimoires: The Secret Grammar of Magic*. Translated by Jon E. Graham. Rochester, VT: Inner Traditions, 2013. Kindle.

———. *Dictionary of Ancient Magic Words and Spells from Abraxas to Zoar*. Translated by Jon E. Graham. Rochester, VT: Inner Traditions, 2015. Kindle.

————. *The High Magic of Talismans and Amulets: Tradition and Craft*. Translated by Jon E. Graham. Rochester, VT: Inner Traditions, 2014. Kindle.

————. *Traditional Magic Spells for Protection and Healing*. Translated by Jon E. Graham. Rochester, VT: Inner Traditions, 2017. Kindle.

Lincoln, Abraham. "Gettysburg Address." Library of Congress. Accessed May 24, 2024. https://www.loc.gov/resource/rbpe.24404500/?st=text.

Lineberry, Cate. "The Worldwide History of Tattoos." *Smithsonian Magazine*. Updated by Sonja Anderson. Updated October 18, 2023. https://www.smithsonianmag.com/history/tattoos-144038580/.

Lundy, Miranda. *Sacred Number: The Secret Qualities of Quantities*. New York: Walker and Co., 2010.

MacLeod, Sharon Paice. *Celtic Cosmology and the Otherworld: Mythic Origins, Sovereignty and Liminality*. Jefferson, NC: McFarland & Company, 2018. Kindle.

Mark, Joshua J. "Ancient Egyptian Writing." World History Encyclopedia. November 16, 2016. https://www.worldhistory.org/Egyptian_Writing/.

Marriott, Susannah. *Witches, Sirens and Soothsayers*. Spruce Books, 2008.

Maxwell-Stuart, Peter. "Magic in the Ancient World." In *The Oxford Illustrated History of Witchcraft and Magic*. Edited by Owen Davies. Oxford, UK: Oxford University Press, 2017.

McTiernan, Jimmy. "Is it Faster to Write in Cursive or Print?" The Productive Engineer. Updated July 27, 2021. https://theproductiveengineer.net/is-it-faster-to-write-in-cursive-or-print.

McWhorter, John. *Ancient Writing and the History of the Alphabet*. Chantilly, VA: The Teaching Company, 2023.

————. *Nine Nasty Words: English in the Gutter: Then, Now, and Forever*. New York: Random House, 2021.

————. *The Story of Human Language*. Chantilly, VA: The Teaching Company, 2004.

Mitchell, Stephen A. *Witchcraft and Magic in the Nordic Middle Ages*. Philadelphia, PA: University of Pennsylvania Press, 2011. Kindle.

Morner, Kathleen, and Ralph Rausch. *NTC's Dictionary of Literary Terms*. Lincolnwood, IL: National Textbook Co., 1991.

"The Neuroscience of Human Vocal Pitch." Cell Press. ScienceDaily. June 28, 2018. www.sciencedaily.com/releases/2018/06/180628151903.htm.

Nims, John Frederick, and David Mason. *Western Wind: An Introduction to Poetry*. 4th ed. Boston, MA: McGraw-Hill, 2000.

Oliver, Mary. *A Poetry Handbook: A Prose Guide to Understanding and Writing Poetry*. New York: Houghton Mifflin, Harcourt Publishing Co., 1994.

Padgett, Ron, ed. *The Teachers & Writers Handbook of Poetic Forms*. 2nd ed. New York: T & W Books, 2000.

Parker, Julia, and Derek Parker. *Parkers' Astrology: The Definitive Guide to Using Astrology in Every Aspect of Your Life*. New York: DK, 2007.

Paxton, Jennifer. *The Celtic World*. Chantilly, VA: The Teaching Company, 2018.

Pesznecker, Susan. *Crafting Magick with Pen and Ink: Learn to Write, Spells and Other Magickal Works*. Woodbury, MN: Llewellyn Publications, 2009. Kindle.

Radin, Dean. *Real Magic: Ancient Wisdom, Modern Science, and a Guide to the Secret Power of the Universe*. New York: Harmony Books, 2018. Kindle.

Robinson, Andrew. *The Story of Writing*. 2nd ed. London: Thames and Hudson, 2020.

Roman Baths. "Roman Curse Tablets." Bath, Somerset. November 2, 2018.

Rowling, J. K. *Harry Potter and the Chamber of Secrets*. New York: Arthur A. Levine Books, 1999.

Schifman, Jonathan. "The Write Stuff: How the Humble Pencil Conquered the World." *Popular Mechanics*. August 16, 2016. https://www.popular mechanics.com/technology/a21567/history-of-the-pencil/.

Sellers, Heather. *The Practice of Creative Writing: A Guide for Students*. 4th ed. Boston, MA: Bedford St. Martin's Press, 2021.

Shlain, Leonard. *The Alphabet Versus the Goddess: The Conflict Between Word and Image*. New York: Penguin Group, 1999.

Sibilia, Mirta, Chiaramaria Stani, Lara Gigli, Simone Pollastri, Alessandro Migliori, Francesco D'Amico, Chiara Schmid et al. "A Multidisciplinary Study Unveils the Nature of a Roman Ink of the I Century AD." *Scientific Reports* 11, no 7231 (March 31, 2021). https://doi.org/10.1038/s41598-021-86288-x.

"Sing." Etymology Online. Accessed July 28, 2023. https://www.etymonline
.com/word/sing.

Skemer, Don C. *Binding Words: Textual Amulets in the Middle Ages*. University
Park: Pennsylvania State University Press, 2006.

"Spell." Etymology Online. Accessed April 2, 2024. https://www.etymonline
.com/word/spell.

Stanborough, Rebecca Joy. "10 Ways That Singing Benefits Your Health."
Healthline. November 10, 2020. https://www.healthline.com/health
/benefits-of-singing.

Starhawk. *The Spiral Dance: A Rebirth of the Ancient Religion of the Great Goddess*.
20th anniversary edition. San Francisco: Harper, 1999.

Strubbe, J. H. M. "Cursed Be He That Moves My Bones." In *Magika Hiera:
Ancient Greek Magic and Religion*, edited by Christopher A. Faraone and Dirk
Obbink. New York: Oxford University Press, 1991.

Strudwick, Helen, ed. *The Encyclopedia of Ancient Egypt*. New York: Metro
Books, 2006.

Swami, Om. *The Ancient Science of Mantras: Wisdom of the Sages*. India: Black
Lotus Press, 2017. Kindle.

Tolkien, J. R. R. "Interview," interview with Denys Gueroult, BBC Radio 4,
Author Archive Collection, 1964, 39:38, June 24, 2014. https://www.bbc
.co.uk/programmes/p021jx7j.

Trafton, Anne. "Singing in the Brain." MIT News. February 22, 2022. https://
news.mit.edu/2022/singing-neurons-0222.

Truss, Lynne. *Eats, Shoots & Leaves*. New York: Gotham Books, 2003.

Wexler, Natalie. "Why Memorizing Stuff Can Be Good for You." *Forbes*. April
29, 2019. https://www.forbes.com/sites/nataliewexler/2019/04/29/why
-memorizing-stuff-can-be-good-for-you/.

Wilburn, Andrew T. *Materia Magica: The Archaeology of Magic in Roman Egypt,
Cyprus, and Spain*. Ann Arbor, MI: University of Michigan Press, 2016.

Whitaker, Hazel. *Palmistry: Your Highway to Life*. Sydney, Australia: Lansdowne
Publishing, 1998.

Whitcomb, Bill. *The Magician's Companion: A Practical & Encyclopedic Guide to
Magical & Religious Symbolism*. St. Paul, MN: Llewellyn Publications, 1999.

"Why Memorizing Things (Though a Lost Art) Isn't a Waste of Time." Cleveland Clinic. September 11, 2018. https://health.clevelandclinic.org/why-memorizing-things-though-a-lost-art-isnt-a-waste-of-time/.

Witchcraft. Edited by Jessica Hundley and Pam Grossman. The Library of Esoterica. Vol. 3. Cologne, Germany: Taschen, 2021.

Wolfe, Joe, Maëva Garnier, and John Smith. "Voice Acoustics: An Introduction." Music Acoustics. University of New South Wales. Accessed April 8, 2024. http://newt.phys.unsw.edu.au/jw/voice.html.

Young, Shinzen. *The Science of Enlightenment: How Meditation Works*. Boulder, CO: Sounds True, 2016.

Zender, Marc. *Writing and Civilization: From Ancient Worlds to Modernity*. Chantilly, VA: The Teaching Company, 2013.

Index

To Write to the Author

If you wish to contact the author or would like more information about this book, please write to the author in care of Llewellyn Worldwide Ltd. and we will forward your request. Both the author and publisher appreciate hearing from you and learning of your enjoyment of this book and how it has helped you. Llewellyn Worldwide Ltd. cannot guarantee that every letter written to the author can be answered, but all will be forwarded. Please write to:

Ember Grant
℅ Llewellyn Worldwide
2143 Wooddale Drive
Woodbury, MN 55125-2989

Please enclose a self-addressed stamped envelope for reply,
or $1.00 to cover costs. If outside the U.S.A., enclose
an international postal reply coupon.

Many of Llewellyn's authors have websites with additional
information and resources. For more information,
please visit our website at http://www.llewellyn.com